Acquired of the Angels

Acquired of the Angels

*The Lives and Works of Master Guitar Makers
John D'Angelico and James L. D'Aquisto*

Second Edition

PAUL WILLIAM SCHMIDT

Scarecrow Press, Inc.
Lanham, Md., and London
1998

SCARECROW PRESS, INC.

Published in the United States of America
by Scarecrow Press, Inc.
4720 Boston Way
Lanham, Maryland 20706

4 Pleydell Gardens
Kent CT20 2DN, England

Copyright © 1998 by Paul William Schmidt

First edition © 1991 by Paul William Schmidt: *Acquired of the Angels: The Lives and Works of Master Guitar Makers John D'Angelico and James L. D'Aquisto.* Metuchen, N.J.: Scarecrow Press. 0-8108-2346-2. All rights reserved. No part of this publication may be reproduced, stored in a retrieval system, or transmitted in any form or by any means, electronic, mechanical, photocopying, recording, or otherwise, without the prior permission of the publisher.

British Library Cataloguing in Publication Information Available

Library of Congress Cataloging-in-Publication Data

Schmidt, Paul William. 1958–
    Acquired of the angels : the lives and works of master guitar makers John D'Angelico and James L. D'Aquisto
by Paul William Schmidt. — 2nd. ed.
      p.   cm.
Includes bibliographical references and index.
ISBN 1-57886-002-4 (cloth : alk. paper)
   1. D'Angelico, John, 1905– . 2. D'Aquisto, James. 3. Guitar makers—United States—Biography.   I. Title.
ML419.D29S3 1998
787.87'19'0922—dc21
[B]
                                                                           98-3052
                                                                             CIP
                                                                             MN

∞™ The paper used in this publication meets the minimum requirements of American National Standard for Information Sciences—Permanence of Paper for Printed Library Materials, ANSI Z39.48–1984.
Manufactured in the United States of America.

Contents

Foreword: Capturing the Magic *Jonathan Kellerman*	vii
Preface	xi
Acknowledgments	xiii
Introduction	1
PART I: D'ANGELICO	3
1. The Man	5
2. The Instruments	27
PART II: D'AQUISTO	77
3. The Man	79
4. The Instruments	103
CONCLUSION: MEMORIES OF THE D'As	137
APPENDIXES	153
The Ledgers	155
D'Angelico Ledger	157
D'Aquisto Ledger	173
SOURCES OF ADDITIONAL INFORMATION	179
INDEX	183
ABOUT THE AUTHOR	185

Foreword: Capturing the Magic

I spotted my first D'Angelico guitar in the pages of a book—one of those old Mel Bay instruction manuals considered *de rigueur* for any schoolboy attempting to scale Mt. Guitar in the fifties—1959, to be exact, well before the Beatles turned everyone on to the joys of the wooden box with six strings. I was nine years old, inspired by the liquid magic of Les Paul's empty-cathedral reverb and lightning arpeggios, the Everly Brothers' ripe-peach harmonies, and Scotty Moore's impeccable rockabilly fills behind the growls and syrup of a young, black-sounding iconoclast named Elvis Presley.

My mother begged me to learn violin. I refused to touch anything but a guitar. The teacher she hired was a stem, northern Italian from Long Island who believed in learning to read music and practicing one hour a day. My prepubescent fingers barely stretched across the fretboard of my Gibson L-30—a pawn shop treasure picked up for $50 by a favorite uncle, near my birthsite on the Lower East Side of Manhattan. An hour-a-day fighting medium-gauge strings and a warped neck hurt like hell, and sometimes I gave up and studied the pictures in the book instead.

And there it was, in glorious black and white: *Mel Bay's own instrument!* Big, blond, curvaceous, festooned with pearl inlay in motifs that evoked the Chrysler building, bottomed by a gleaming, engraved, outrageously angled metal tailpiece that made my guitar's chrome trapezoid resemble a hardware-store castoff.

D'Angelico. Even the name on the multi-bound headstock sounded glamorous—redolent of nightclubs and sleek, black cars, white-toothed women with long legs, and clinking glasses.

It was 1980 when I actually got to play and purchase a D'Angelico guitar—a 1953 noncutaway, sunburst New Yorker. By then I'd heard of the D'A mystique, but it wasn't until I strummed and picked *and felt* the lacquered box vibrating next to my body, experienced those pulsing, throbbing chords, round notes, and sweet sustain, that I appreciated the reality of what a little bachelor laboring in a small shop—*on the Lower East Side of Manhattan!*—had accomplished.

Since then, I've played and owned scores of D'Angelicos and D'Aquistos, as well as Strombergs, Wilkanowskis, Maccaferis, Epiphones, Gibsons, and Martins. Each one is different, all are wonderful. But D'Angelicos and D'Aquistos are special.

The consistency of John D'Angelico and James D'Aquisto's work is beyond impressive. Occasionally, one hears grousing about "dogs" created by the masters. In nearly every case, the complaints result from improper care and setup and *inadequate use*. For, more than any other type of guitar, carved-tops respond to playing, much in the way that children respond to attention. Neglect an instrument and it closes up, withdraws, reduces itself to something tight and unyielding. A well-played D'Angelico or D'Aquisto is nearly inevitably a joy.

If a cardinal trait of D'Angelico guitars must be singled out, I'd choose *sweetness*. Other brands may achieve it, but rarely with the uniformity and to the extent of the 1,164 masterpieces created by D'Angelico.

I've found D'Aquistos to be lighter, crisper, more precise, spookily balanced, most often possessing a lovely, piano-like bass. Jimmy experimented and took risks, nearly always successfully. At his best, he was beyond description.

He was also a gentleman. He and I corresponded by mail during the 1980s. I was attempting to learn more about the provenance of the D'Angelicos in my possession—date of manufacture, original purchasers, design of pickguards, and that sort of thing. This was before the publication of books such as this one, and later works authored by George Gruhn, Akira Tsumura, and Scott Chinery, and information was sketchy, at best. Jimmy was my only link to the past, and, though busy with his own projects, he came through promptly and generously, going so far as to sketch pickguard designs.

A few years later, I met him at a NAMM show in Orange County, California. He'd already achieved living-legend status and I was surprised at how young and fit he looked. Despite feeling lousy. For that day, he was reeling from the effects of a severe grand mal epileptic seizure, the disorder that would eventually take his life.

Jimmy D'Aquisto was a genius.

John D'Angelico was a genius.

Both died at the age of 59, leaving us only to wonder about what might have been.

This book captures the magic. The original edition was a landmark publication: the first time anyone had attempted to illuminate, in depth, the lives and work of these two remarkable artists. I remember picking up the book, reading a bit, thinking, "Yes! He got it right!"

Paul Schmidt writes with exceptional clarity, elegance, and that special grace that separates the pros from the amateurs. *Acquired of the Angels* goes beyond facts and figures and cold biography, and succeeds by dint of scholarliness, talent, and affection, in evoking the glorious essences of its subjects.

This is an important book.

And now, in its second edition, it is even more superb, augmented by additional photos, including some beautiful color shots, and the addition of new—tragically post mortem—material on Jimmy D'Aquisto.

Read it and weep, for masters long departed.

Read it and smile, for the enduring beauty they left behind.

JONATHAN KELLERMAN
Beverly Hills, California

Preface

As a boy, I saw a British film version of Dickens's *A Christmas Carol* and was deeply moved by a particular scene. As Scrooge ended his time with the Ghost of Christmas Present, the ghost opened his robe, revealing two urchins, one male and one female. Scrooge inquired whose they were, upon which the phantom replied, "They are Man's. . . . This boy is Ignorance. This girl is Want. Beware them both . . . but most of all beware this boy." The book in your hands is one of my labors in bewaring the boy.

In addition to my altruistic intent of quelling ignorance, I must confess that there was another (somewhat selfish) reason for undertaking the project: I wanted to read a book like this but could not find one.

As my musical life and education flourished I became terribly interested in the arch-top guitar and its acoustic capabilities. My inquiries led me to John D'Angelico's guitars, and I soon realized that there was little in print regarding the man and his works. I found it odd that one could be so lauded and yet remain so unresearched and undocumented.

While in graduate school in the late 1970s I became acquainted with Tim Olsen and Jon Peterson from the Guild of American Luthiers, and they were the ones who first introduced me to James D'Aquisto's role in the D'Angelico legacy. After visiting with James D'Aquisto in 1982, I realized that he was perhaps the last truly credible link with D'Angelico, and given that he represented the evolution of the D'Angelico ethic, it struck me that a project such as this needed to be done—both for its historical importance and for the artistic soul of humanity. I asked Mr. D'Aquisto if I could carry out this venture with his blessing and assistance, and he agreed.

To be certain, this project would never have come to fruition had it not been for Mr. D'Aquisto, not only as a subject but also as the most important source of knowledge, information, and insight. John D'Angelico was a very private man. Only two persons worked with him for any length of time: Vincent DiSerio and James L. D'Aquisto. When I began this project, Mr. DiSerio had long since died, leaving Jimmy D'Aquisto as the single intimate, reliable source capable of reconstructing a plausible account of the working career of John D'Angelico. Other information was gathered from discussions with veteran musicians, informed and experienced dealers and collectors of guitars, other guitar scholars, family members, peers of D'Angelico and D'Aquisto, and my own studied perceptions.

The second part of this book, on Mr. D'Aquisto, was at once easier and more difficult to compile and organize than the D'Angelico section. When the first edition of this book was published in 1991, the D'Angelico story was already finite—what had been lost to scholarship had been lost. But Mr. D'Aquisto was still working and creating exemplary musical tools, and his work was ever full of newness: fresh discoveries were still occurring at every turn, nuanced perceptions were constantly ripening—it was the nature of his being, and the instruments were testaments to the same.

When Mr. D'Aquisto died suddenly in the spring of 1995, the first edition of this book became incomplete, and after some natural grieving on my part, I felt that it was important to complete the story. Now, as when I first began this project in the early 1980s, it is still my sincerest hope that this publication might provide the opportunity to continually introduce these fine artists to new generations and that their stories may in some way continually inspire kindred spirits to transcend convention and nourish authenticity.

Acknowledgments

The following persons were instrumental in helping to organize this project. Some individuals provided a great deal of help—supportive letters, photographs, interviews, etc.—while others helped in other ways. I am thankful for all provisions, great and small. They are listed alphabetically.

Chris Ambadjes, Steven Andersen, Billy Bauer, Fr. Robert Bauer, Bill Bay, Mel Bay, Robert Bein, Dick Boak, Harold Bradley, Jack Brostrom, Alexander Calder, Mike Carey, Lou Catello, Mark Cleary, Frederick Cohen, Fr. Jim Colopy, Mary D'Aquisto, Phyllis D'Aquisto, Glen Delman, Don Demarco, Lonni Elrod, Darwin Evans, Phillip Fairbanks, Frog (Steve Forgey), Artie Foster, GPI Publications, Ray Gogarty, George Gruhn, Paul Gudelsky, Norman Harris, Jerry Haussler, W. E. Hill & Sons, Dr. Thomas Martin Horning, Amanda Irwin, Stan Jay, Dexter Johnson, Michael Katz, Dr. Jonathan Kellerman, Skip Kelly, Steve Klein, Joe Lalaina, Shirley Lambert, Gary Larson, Frank Lucido, Dean Lueking, Josh McClure, Phyllis McVey, George Melega, Thom Merton, Lynn Montague, John Monteleone, D. Gregory Nelson, Katherine Neubauer, Sherri Oliver, Tim Olsen, Joe Patire, Carl Patterson, Jon Peterson, Bucky Pizzarelli, Tom Ribbecke, Sal Salvador, Jo Dee Schmidt (my more-than-loving wife), Haley Schmidt, Luke Schmidt, Anne Schmidt, Peter Schmidt, Gretchen Schmidt, Warren and Mary Schmidt, David Sebring, Johnny Smith, David C. Smith, Matt Umanov, Maurice Utrillo, Al Valenti, Pete Wagener, Lynn Weber, Stan Werbin, Lawrence B. Wexer, Tom Wheeler, John Wilkens, Neil Young.

Introduction

John D'Angelico and James L. D'Aquisto were artists. Their works happen to be usable in a more pragmatic way than, say, a painting by Rembrandt or a sculpture by Michelangelo, but their essence is the same. In a format such as this book provides, detailing the concrete aspects of their lives and works is far simpler than capturing their artistry. Yet it is the latter that is of much greater significance in grasping the wonder of these men and their creations. The building of one's "self" into an instrument is incalculable, yet it is that element that is of paramount importance in discussing and understanding the "D'As." To speak of art as a system or method is to speak of things that cannot merge. Indeed, art is more like the element mercury than it is like steel or clay, and it can only be created by those who are doing what they were created to do. D'Angelico and D'Aquisto trusted their intuition, about their life's vocation and about all of the details of their instruments. And in so doing they not only raised and deepened the art of guitar-making but also reminded us of some important perspectives on how to invest one's life.

PART I

D'Angelico

D'Angelico Means "Of the Angels"

Photo of John D'Angelico at 40 Kenmare Street in 1932 as it hung in the D'Aquisto shop. *(Photo courtesy of the author's archive.)*

1
The Man

John D'Angelico was born in New York City in 1905, the first child of four, to a family from Naples, Italy. In 1914, at the age of nine, he became apprenticed to his granduncle Ciani. The Ciani shop, located on Kenmare Street in New York, created violins, mandolins, and flat-top guitars and made repairs on these and similar instruments. There is little verifiable information about the details of his boyhood, but it would be safe to conjecture that it was not unlike that of many young apprenticed males of the day: hard work, long hours, and little pay.

When his granduncle died, D'Angelico took over supervision of the shop and its dozen or so workers, even though he was still in his teens. It was during this period that he began the study of violin-playing and violin-making with a local artist named Mario Frosali. D'Angelico eventually tired of working for his aunt, as the roles of employee and supervisor were not confluent with his true desires. Thus, at the age of twenty-seven he opened his own shop at 40 Kenmare Street.

Initially D'Angelico employed three or four persons, most of whom were immigrant woodworkers. These workers did not stay long, however, and soon the D'Angelico shop consisted only of D'Angelico and his assistant, Vincent DiSerio. D'Angelico was still studying violin-making with Frosali when he first opened shop, and his first instruments were violins, mandolins, and arch-top f-hole guitars patterned after the Lloyd Loar Gibson L-5 guitar. In a manner of speaking, D'Angelico's first fruits were "Gibsons" made by D'Angelico. Soon, however, he began incorporating his knowledge and experience from the Ciani shop, the violin-making study with Frosali, and his own experimentation, to produce authentically "D'Angelico" guitars. D'Angelico always had great respect for Gibson instruments and always watched what the company produced. Indeed, he had a wealth of experience with Gibsons and the then-popular Epiphone instruments as well, as he not only made his own instruments but also did work on guitars, violins, mandolins, basses, and banjos. He also took trades and in later days sold new Favilla guitars (made by Frank Favilla) and Ampeg amplifiers.

Perhaps the most popular guitars of the day were Gibsons, and obviously D'Angelico could not compete in terms of business. In the first years of his shop, D'Angelico routinely worked seven days a week and into the early morning hours, merely to complete more instruments and get them out so that others might

Al Valenti and John D'Angelico in front of D'Angelico's shop with a New Yorker in the summer of 1938. *(Photo courtesy of Al Valenti.)*

Kenmare Street in New York as it appeared in 1997. *(Photo courtesy of Michael Katz.)*

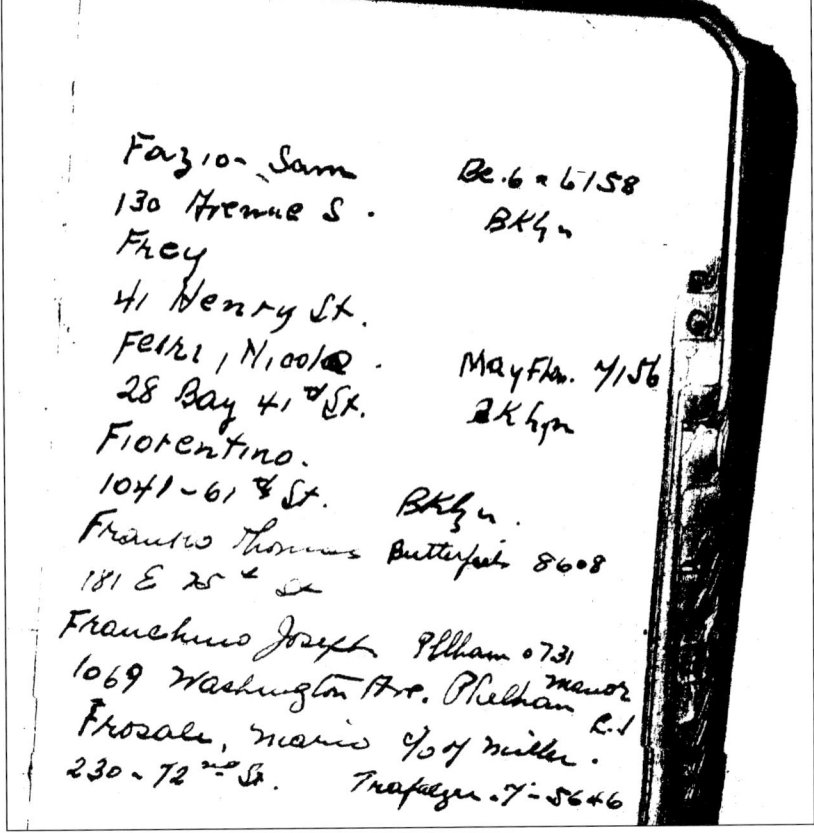

D'Angelico's ledger book with addresses. Note the last entry of his violin instructor Mario Frosali. *(Photo courtesy of the author's archive and James D'Aquisto.)*

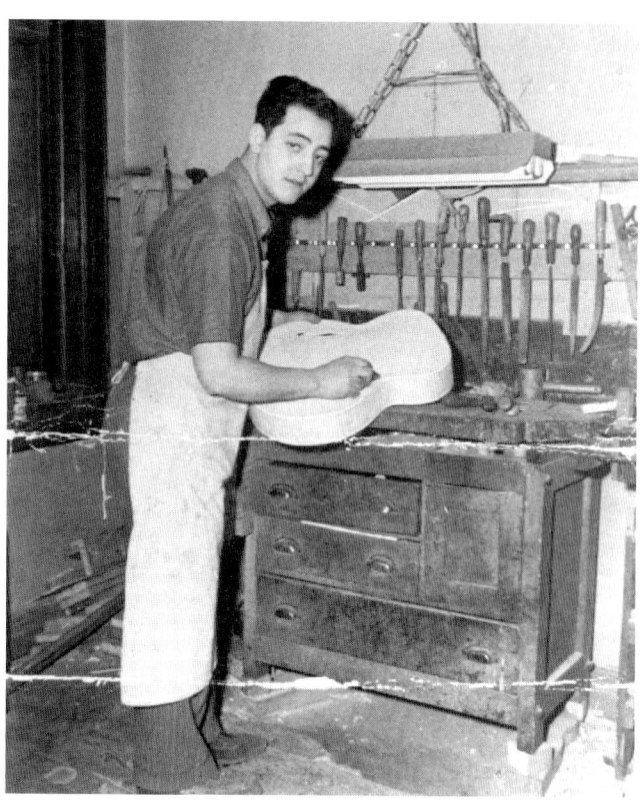

Vincent DiSerio
(Photo courtesy of Vincent DiSerio and the author's archive.)

John D'Angelico contouring a neck. Note the unfinished mandolins and the noncutaway forms.
(Photo courtesy of Vincent DiSerio and the author's archive.)

know of them. Occasionally D'Angelico would sell instruments to musical instrument dealers such as Gravois Music, Newcorn Music, and Silver & Horland. They were priced as Gibsons, and they were sold on their quality.

As his instruments became known and the demand for them increased, D'Angelico elected to continue making them one at a time by hand. D'Aquisto recalled:

> He had the experience of having people working for him in the early days, and he wanted no part of that ever again. He had no desire to be a big manufacturer at all. In the 1940s Fred Gretsch [president of the Gretsch Manufacturing Co., a prominent maker of musical instruments at that time] wanted John to close up shop and come and work for him. Gretsch told John that he could be in charge of all of the details of the entire guitar production. John would have nothing to do with it. Money and building a reputation and being famous were the farthest things from his mind. John wanted to keep the instruments his own.

Keeping the instruments "his own" is precisely the reason that they were what they were. D'Angelico worked with players in the sense that he was willing to do (within limits) what a customer wanted. Players who wanted special attention and special features came to D'Angelico—for cosmetic variations or for the sound that only D'Angelico could create.

Surprisingly, D'Angelico was not a guitar player, though he considered the guitar to be the ultimate instrument. His personal taste in music leaned toward the chord/melody style played by Benny Mortel and his close friend and promoter Alphonse Valenti; he also favored Django Reinhardt and his work with Stéphane Grappelli. He was not fond of the bop or "cool" styles that became popular in the 1940s and 1950s.

D'Angelico was a private man, preferring his work and the company of his friends and his family. He never married. Often he would break from his work in the early afternoon by taking a walk in downtown Manhattan, frequenting the hardware stores

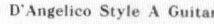

Promotional announcement for a demonstration of D'Angelico's Excel by Al Valenti, 1935. *(Photo courtesy of Al Valenti and the author's archive.)*

Al Valenti with early D'Angelico 16-inch noncutaway Excel-style A-style guitars, 1934. *(Photo courtesy of Al Valenti and the author's archive.)*

and tool-making and machine shops; he would typically return with a number of new gadgets. He was not a traveler; the farthest anyone remembers him traveling was out to Elizabeth, New Jersey, to United Guitars, which was owned by Frank Forcillo—a friend and one of the original workers in the D'Angelico shop. D'Angelico's friend Ray Gogarty recalls the time John went on a boating excursion: "For John it was like a trip to Europe!" Many of the fine players who commissioned an instrument from D'Angelico concur that he was generous, friendly, and uncompromisingly scrupulous in his work. Jazz guitarist Johnny Smith recalled:

> I got to know John and the friendship was immediate. He wasn't an especially outgoing person, but if he liked you he was very warm. I felt fortunate to call him a friend. He was very open

```
                                                    Telephone CAnal 6-2524
MAKER
  of            JOHN D'ANGELICO
 Fine
GUITARS         40 KENMARE STREET ... NEW YORK 12, N.Y.
```

Oct. 3rd 1955

Ray Gogarty
102 East Shore drive
Massapequa, L.I.

Dear Ray;

Recieved your letter and was nice to hear from you. I see you are becoming quite an authority on neck adjustments, I don't blame you, you need to be especially if you are near water.

I can see the problem you have according to your sketch, this has happened to me time and time again, there is no trick to tightening them except, as you give it quarter turns at a time, squint your eye along the edge of the fingerboard, especially along the treble side, and to stop, as soon as you see a bulge in any part along the fingerboard. That snake like affect usually happens on all makes, some more and some less. We have tried to elimate it on our guitar, by placing the truce rod just a little different than others, which I feel works a little better, than any other truss rod on the market.

To eliminate this snake like warpings, the only solution is a new fret job, by doing this we have a chance to straighten the fingerboard wood, or if very bad a new fingerboard is a must.

Hope I have made myself clear, Ray. If you get a chance stop down to see us.

Regards to the gang.

Very truly yours,

John D'Angelico

Regards from Jimmie.

Letter from D'Angelico to friend and customer Ray Gogarty. (*Courtesy of Ray Gogarty and the author's archive.*)

THE MAN 13

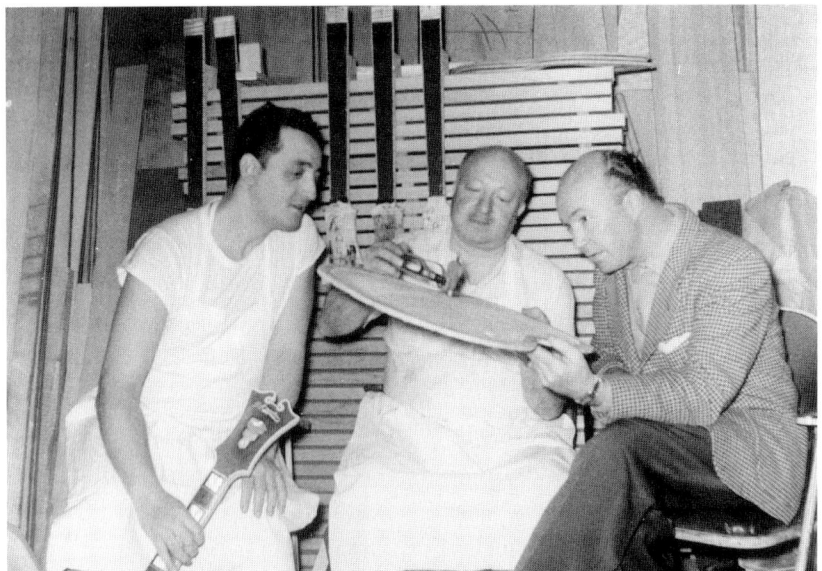

From left: DiSerio, D'Angelico, and Ray Gogarty (guitarist and friend of D'Angelico).
(Photo courtesy of Ray Gogarty.)

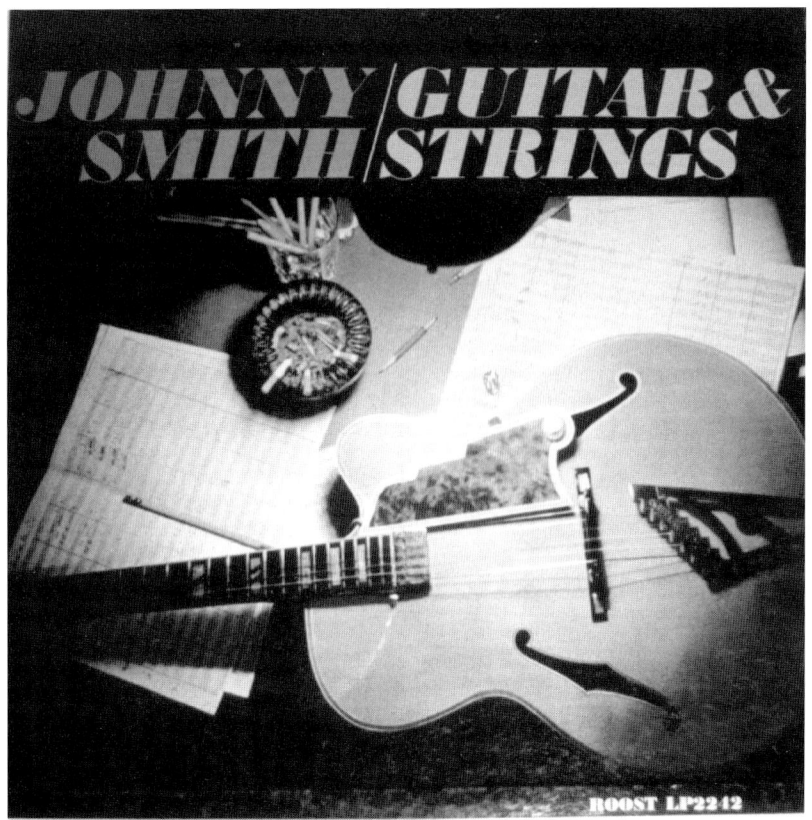

Johnny Smith's D'Angelico gracing the cover of one of his many albums. This photo was taken between refinishings, thus the blond top.
(Photo courtesy of Peter Schmidt and the author's archive.)

about his work—he'd always show me what he was doing and explain how and why he was doing it. I was astounded by his ability—a true, absolute-perfection artist. I was very privileged to know this great master.

D'Angelico would do his utmost to please those who sought him out, but he was quick to call things as they were. He was intolerant of those who attempted to treat him condescendingly or who made inappropriate demands. Temperamental perhaps, but never eccentric, D'Angelico could display a "just anger," as D'Aquisto noted:

I'd see someone walk in the shop, and watch John literally throw them out like a lunatic. Then I'd hear the story and it would make sense. I remember one instance when a woman brought in an old mandolin that was nearly in pieces. John repaired it to the point of almost better than new. Well, the woman came in to pick up the mandolin and all of a sudden I

John D'Angelico in his shop on Kenmare Street in the late 1950s. *(Photo courtesy of Ray Gogarty.)*

heard John screaming—so I came running into the room to see him waving the mandolin around, threatening to put it back the way it was. Jimmy [the nickname of Vincent DiSerio] and I grabbed him and gave the woman her mandolin and told her to just leave. When we got John calmed down he told us that the woman had pointed at a little scratch and said, "I don't remember that being there," with a real attitude. Here he had taken this mandolin that was almost completely destroyed and made it right, and the appreciation he got was a petty remark about a little scratch.

Neither was the young D'Aquisto exempt from reproof:

One of my jobs was to hand-buff the guitars. I used to sand the spray off, then I'd hand-buff it to bring up the gloss. I did it that way for about six years until finally John bought a buffer. When it was still new to me I thought I had it down cold.

A fellow came to pick up his guitar, which had been in for a repair, and it was all strung-up and ready to go. He had one of those silk-like cords some of the players used as a strap back then, with a tassel at the end. John saw a little mark on the guitar and told me to buff it out. So I turned on the machine and John warned me to take the tassel off because it might get stuck in the machine. I told him not to worry about it, that I had it down cold.

Sure enough, the wheel grabs the strap and takes the guitar out of my hands, spins it around, and the guitar comes back and smashes me on the head and proceeds to fly fifteen feet across the room and hits the far wall, and falls to the floor in pieces. John starts screaming, "You sonuvabitch, I told you to take the damn strap off! Good, I hope you broke your head, you deserve it!" John was raving. He went into the showroom and took a brand new Favilla out of the case, handed it to the fellow that had just watched his guitar get demolished, and said, "Don't worry about it, he'll pay for it. I'll take it out of his salary." He never did take a cent out of my salary.

D'Angelico also had a great sense of humor. D'Aquisto remembered one example:

> John was always doing stunts, like pretending someone tripped him and looking around—the Marx Brothers type of humor. One time a fellow came in to get his guitar and John did a fake fall onto this old "junker" guitar that someone from the neighborhood had given him—a beat-up old Stella or something. John and Jimmy started stepping on the guitar and crunched it to bits. All the while the customer is thinking it's his instrument, as John pretends to be upset and offers apologies all over the place; the guy was turning pale. When John finally explained it was a joke, the guy wanted to kill him. That was John.

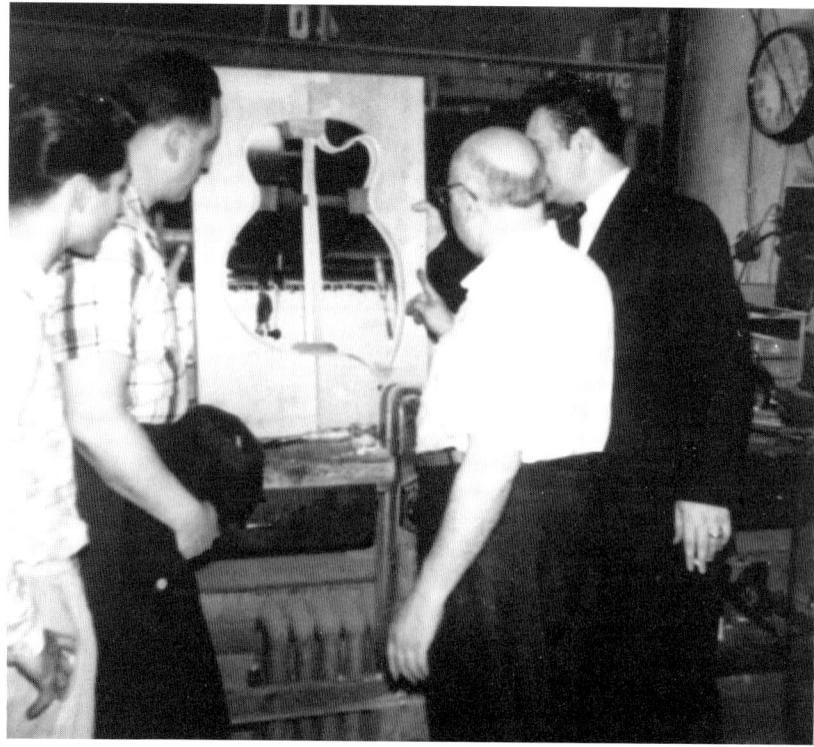

From left: Jimmy D'Aquisto, Vincent DiSerio, John D'Angelico, and Peter Girardi (a customer). *(Photo courtesy of John Monteleone Archive.)*

John D'Angelico and Vincent DiSerio. *(Photo courtesy of Ray Gogarty.)*

D'Angelico's shop was located in a relatively new five-story building on Kenmare Street. He rented the shop on street level (40 Kenmare) and the apartment on the top floor (36 Kenmare). The shop had originally been a bank and consisted of one large room. D'Aquisto described the room as follows:

> As you walked into the shop there was the bench and counter on the left, and to the right was a wall of pictures with all of the fellows that played his guitars. Then about ten feet ahead there was a showcase with Favilla guitars and secondhand guitars that he took on trade for his.

In the early 1950s D'Angelico obtained a little store next to his shop, broke through the wall, and turned the newly acquired space into his showroom. One of D'Aquisto's first jobs as an apprentice after joining D'Angelico in 1952 was to help make and upholster the racks inside the cases where the new Favilla guitars, new United guitars, and secondhand instruments were stored. Behind the showcases there was a long counter and a few amplifiers (D'Angelico sold Nathan Daniel's Danelectro amplifiers and Everett Hull's Ampeg amplifiers), and at the back there was a desk. The environment for creating D'Angelico instruments remained relatively unchanged for twenty-seven years—a functional, unobtrusive atmosphere.

The year 1959 was a difficult one for D'Angelico. The building in which he lived and worked had been built directly above a city water main, which broke in 1959. As a result of that breakage the building's foundation shifted such that the entire structure began falling forward—so much so that it threatened to topple. The building was condemned and the fifty-four-year-old artist who had built his world at 40 Kenmare Street was forced to move from his home and workplace. Obviously, his first priority was to find a dwelling, and he moved in with his brother-in-law and

John D'Angelico working on an instrument in the 1950s. *(Photo courtesy of Ray Gogarty.)*

THE MAN 19

Al Valenti demonstrating the D'Angelico guitar and Danelectro amplifiers (which D'Angelico sold in his shop) at the music trade show and convention at the New Yorker Hotel in New York City, July 25–28, 1949. *(Photo courtesy of Al Valenti.)*

nephew, who lived nearby. The young D'Aquisto saw his mentor emotionally crushed. It was also at this time, D'Aquisto recalled, that Vincent DiSerio split with D'Angelico:

> At first we began looking around town, and the rents were outrageous. Finally we ended up on 24th Street, where an old school had been turned into a factory. Emmanuel Valesquez [a maker of fine classical guitars] was there and he'd figured John could get one of the lofts. Well, on the way home from that visit, John and Vincent got into a violent argument about money, and when we dropped off John, they were clear that they'd never have anything to do with one another again. You see, all along DiSerio wanted John to turn the place into a manufacturing-type operation, a company like Gibson or Epiphone. He wanted to make the guitars faster so we could earn more money. He wasn't that interested in the artistic aspect of it. John and I both agreed with DiSerio that we should be getting more money for the instruments than we were, but we thought we had to stay in line with what Gibson was charging, so we never made much money.

Vincent DiSerio had begun working for D'Angelico at the shop's inception in 1932 at the age of twelve. The young DiSerio performed typical apprentice activities, such as sweeping up, taking necks to the engraver, and picking up tuners. He began working on the guitars in earnest after returning from the army at the close of World War II.

DiSerio's work represented a great deal of the D'Angelico process. It was his job to draw the templates for the backs and other pieces on large blocks of wood and then cut them out on the band saw. He was also to cut out the mass necks and put the rods in them, glue the extra pieces on either side of the headpiece, cut out the fingerboards and incise the lines into them in preparation for the frets, glue the fingerboards on the necks, and perform similar functions.

D'Angelico did the more refined tasks, such as shaping the fingerboards and placing the frets into them, carving the tops and backs, dovetailing, and fashioning other fine details. Once those procedures were completed by D'Angelico, DiSerio would sand the exterior of the back, sides, and neck, put the inlay into the fingerboard and headpiece (excluding the name D'Angelico), place the binding around the edges and the f-holes, and put the first coat of lacquer on the entire instrument. D'Angelico was certainly capable of these tasks, as he had done them himself in earlier years, but assigning these duties to DiSerio hastened the completion of an instrument and allowed D'Angelico to concentrate on the more artistic and refined aspects of the process. DiSerio, however, was not capable of the intricate tasks D'Angelico performed.

DiSerio played a very important role in the creation of D'Angelico instruments from the mid-1940s through the late 1950s. He was responsible for improvements and alterations in designs relating to his labors, and he taught the young D'Aquisto the "rough" work involved in arch-top construction.

Upon leaving D'Angelico, DiSerio took a position at the Favilla guitar shop, working in the production line (by this time being run by Herk Favilla, Frank's younger brother, as Frank had died). In later days he handcrafted his own flat-top classical cutaway guitars, but he did not make arch-top guitars. Sadly, the rift between D'Angelico and DiSerio was never resolved.

Meanwhile, though D'Angelico had signed a lease on 24th Street, there was still no shop. Months passed with no activity and in order to support himself, the young D'Aquisto began playing bass and guitar in local nightclubs—a life he detested. D'Aquisto was desperate to get back to guitar-making and even contacted DiSerio for a prospective position at the Favilla shop. D'Aquisto remembers DiSerio as being unhelpful, worsening D'Aquisto's discouragement. D'Aquisto then attempted to stir D'Angelico:

> I called John up and said, "Bo [the nickname used for D'Angelico], what are you doing? Let's open up the shop! You're just sitting around being depressed and it's not doing

either of us any good!" He said he was tired and disgusted and that he'd had enough. Well, across from the old shop there was this little one-story store that was a wholesale coffee specialty shop that was going out of business. The store was half the size of John's shop—about the size of my shop now—and John wasn't used to working in that small of an area. I kept trying to talk him into it, but he was still down about everything. I stayed at him and we got some guys to put in a suspended floor above, where we could store the wood. We took two of the showcases and brought them into the little shop, and that picture of John and myself standing in front of the shop is that little shop. We set up the machinery the way my shop is set up now. We set up the benches in front of the two front windows.

We moved all of the machinery in the dead of winter with the help of two neighborhood friends. John got pneumonia from the move and eventually wound up in the hospital. "Well," said John, "I guess we'll mostly do repairs. DiSerio's not here now and I can't do all of the work he was doing, and I'd have to teach you all over . . ." and I interrupted him and said, "What are you talking about? Who do you think was doing all of the work anyway?" He was surprised. He didn't know that I was capable of doing all of the work DiSerio was doing, as well as the fine detail work I was already doing. So when he saw that I could do the work, we started to make guitars again. Then, I slowly began doing work DiSerio hadn't attempted—carving the tops and backs, bending the sides, shaping the necks, all of that. It was a blessing for me when DiSerio left because I was sort of demanding of John, because I wanted to learn all of the things he did.

Thus, the instruments produced from 1960 through 1964 were made by both D'Angelico and D'Aquisto. The instruments continued to become more refined musically and fancier visually: more layers of bindings, bigger headpieces, more pearl, and so forth. It was during this period that D'Aquisto learned the finer skills of guitar-making and grew ever closer to D'Angelico.

It was also during this period that D'Angelico's health failed drastically. Between pneumonia, repeated heart attacks, and a legacy in

Photo of John D'Angelico and James D'Aquisto in front of the new shop at 37 Kenmare Street, circa 1960, as it hung in D'Aquisto's shop. *(Photo courtesy of the author's archive.)*

the D'Angelico family of not reaching the seventh decade of life, the inevitable was imminent. D'Aquisto remembered the end:

> I went down to the shop one day and it was still closed. He had already had three heart attacks and I was worried. I walked to his brother-in-law's, and his brother-in-law opened the door. I saw John's brother Alfred there and he looked at me and said, "John's dead." He had died in his sleep. I saw John lying there in his bed. I couldn't believe it.

John D'Angelico died on Tuesday, September 1, 1964, at the age of fifty-nine. His obituary ran in that Thursday's *New York Times*. It read as follows:

> John D'Angelico, a well-known guitar maker, died Tuesday of a heart ailment in his home at 166 Mulberry Street. His age was 59.
>
> In his small instrument shop at 37 Kenmare Street, Mr. D'Angelico had made as many as 10 orchestral arch-topped guitars a year. His customers willingly waited 10 or 20 years to possess one.
>
> Despite the demand for his instruments, he would often charge only what his customer could afford to pay or would give a guitar away to a person who truly appreciated it.
>
> A short, modest and cheerful man, he often worked 16 hours a day. He was born near his store and learned his craft 40 years ago from a granduncle who first made mandolins and then guitars.
>
> Mr. D'Angelico also made some violins and mandolins, and repaired these instruments as well as guitars, but the making of fine guitars was his obsession. His guitars were sought by guitarists of leading orchestras.
>
> A brother, Alfred, survives.

Sadly, the obituary was replete with errors. D'Angelico made far more than ten instruments a year; in his thirty-plus years of creating he made 1,164 numbered guitars, as well as violins, mandolins, novelty instruments, and plywood electric guitars. The normal waiting time was only several months, although in later years some did wait as long as two years. And D'Angelico did not give instruments away, nor did he make concessions as to the selling price.

He was laid to rest in a family grave in Calvary Cemetery, Queens, New York. The one tombstone for the entire family, simply reads "D'Angelico"—no first names, no dates, no details, no epitaph.

D'Angelico's obituary as it ran in the *New York Times*.

JOHN D'ANGELICO, 59, A MAKER OF GUITARS

John D'Angelico, a well-known guitar maker, died Tuesday of a heart ailment in his home at 166 Mulberry Street. His age was 59.

In his small instrument shop at 37 Kenmare Street, Mr. D'Angelico had made as many as 10 orchestral or arch-topped guitars a year. His customers willingly waited 10 or 20 years to possess one.

Despite the demand for his instruments, he would often charge only what his customer could afford to pay or would give a guitar away to a person who truly appreciated it.

A short, modest and cheerful man, he often worked 16 hours a day. He was born near his store and learned his craft 40 years ago from a granduncle who first made mandolins and then guitars.

Mr. D'Angelico also made some violins and mandolins, and repaired these instruments as well as guitars, but the making of fine guitars was his obsession. His guitars were sought by guitarists of leading orchestras.

A brother, Alfred, survives.

The Instruments

The carved top and back design is the latest evolutionary step in acoustic guitar construction; yet, as such, it is often poorly understood. For most of the twentieth century, these instruments have been viewed either as "rhythm" instruments or as instruments that are to be used with an electric pickup. It is of course understandable why these perceptions flourish: arch-tops were often used to play rhythm-style chords (most notably in jazz and big bands) and were then popularized with pickups attached. Though carved-top guitars are acoustic instruments, many are viewed as having a harsh or "steely" tone, limiting their usefulness in certain situations. That harshness may be an accurate descriptive for many arch-tops (and indeed a feature for some applications), but D'Angelicos and D'Aquistos are different.

Ignorance about the musical suitability of "D'As" is both common and understandable. It is quite simply very difficult to try out a D'Angelico or D'Aquisto instrument: they are rarely available for resale (and when they are, the cost is typically prohibitive for most players); perhaps fewer than a thousand persons in the world own them. Thus, ignorance, limited availability, reticence of players from other styles to experiment, and cost all contribute to some of the misunderstandings surrounding some of the twentieth century's finest guitars.

What is it about D'Angelicos that caused (and still causes) such a stir? Indeed, there flocked to John D'Angelico a veritable aviary of musicians, who were to fly all over guitaristic life in New York and throughout the world. Certainly there was something extraordinary about this man's creations.

Headpiece of the second D'Angelico ever made. *(Photo courtesy of John Monteleone Archive.)*

Headpiece of a style-B instrument. *(Photo courtesy of Tom Wheeler.)*

Headpiece of a noncutaway instrument from the early 1940s, #1551. This example is unusual, as the back and the neck are fashioned from mahogany. *(Photo courtesy of John Monteleone Archive.)*

Headpiece of a 1953 New Yorker. (Photo courtesy of Mark Cleary.)

AIMS IN RELATION TO TONE

Speaking of an instrument's tone is not unlike speaking of artistry—it is subjective and abstract and therefore the most interesting and most important factor in any musical tool. To be certain, considerations such as action and feel and the appearance of an instrument are important—but the sound of an instrument is its soul.

Workmanship, materials, and design are the significant hallmarks of any instrument, design being by far the most important aspect. Both D'Angelico and D'Aquisto strove to create responsive musical tools, and that responsiveness manifested itself in the form of balance, sustain, clarity, articulation, and a certain smoothness that owners and players continually attempt to quantify. Rich, thick, resonant, clear, bright, loud, soft, round, producing pear-shaped notes, bell-like without being shrill or metallic—all of these apply. The gradations of tone colors are as varied as the instruments themselves.

Basic differences such as body size and depth, scale length, size and type of bridge, shape of the carved top, neck angle, internal bracing pattern, type of strings, and so on, all lend another dimension to the tone of an instrument. The way an instrument is setup also directly impacts its performance: it is possible to experience a superior instrument that has not been intelligently attended to and be less than thrilled—a situation not unlike test-driving an exceptional automobile that is in need of an engine adjustment, and then dismissing it as inferior.

Another important subtlety that affects the tone is how a particular instrument is played; one can actually play a sound into an instrument. If there were two identical D'Angelicos (which there are not) and one were played with a heavy pick, rhythm-style, and the other played gently, finger-style, as the years progressed the differences in those instruments would become more and more apparent. Playing an instrument gives it character, and the style one plays directly affects that character.

There are differences of opinion, but many acknowledge that there are perhaps no makers who have created instruments that surpass the balance, sustain, projection, and tonal character of D'Angelico and D'Aquisto arch-top guitars. Experienced New York dealer Matt Umanov perceived, "You cannot talk about any other guitars in the same breath as D'Angelico and D'Aquisto. They're in another galaxy."

D'ANGELICO'S FIRST FRUITS

I have elected to begin with the instruments that bore the D'Angelico name, rather than the instruments he had a hand in creating during his association with the Ciani shop. Research of the latter provided mercilessly sketchy and unreliable clues as to what the young D'Angelico did or did not do. There are, however, verifiable reports by D'Angelico's contemporaries, such as Al Valenti, who recall D'Angelico creating several arch-top guitars in the late 1920s for those that requested them; but D'Angelico did not begin to create arch-tops in earnest until he opened his shop at 40 Kenmare Street in 1932.

D'Angelico had worked with stringed instruments for eighteen years prior to opening his own shop. When he first began making instruments on his own, he made violins, mandolins, and arch-top guitars styled after the Lloyd Loar Gibson L-5. The L-5 was introduced to the public in 1924, though it was in production by 1923. It featured a 16¼-inch body (measured at the lower bout), a 24¾-inch scale length, a brown sunburst finish, unbound f-holes, an elevated finger-rest, an adjustable bridge, steel strings, a fourteen-fret neck/body joint, an adjustable truss rod, and celluloid binding around the top, back, peghead, and finger-rest. It had an ebony fingerboard with pearl position markers, a three-piece maple neck, a carved maple back, maple sides, and a carved spruce top (L-5s from 1923 had birch backs). D'Angelico copied that design almost exactly, save the truss rod, as Gibson had a patent on that feature.

Many people referred to (and still refer to) the arch-top f-hole guitar as a "jazz" guitar, as the design became so closely associated

The second D'Angelico ever made. This instrument was completely restored by luthier John Monteleone, who received it in pieces in a paper bag. The pickguard is not original, nor is the bridge, although the original bridge remains intact—it is of very light construction, almost dainty. The date (November 28, 1932) and the serial number (1002) are written in pen inside the instrument on the back, and both are barely legible.
(Photo courtesy of John Monteleone Archive.)

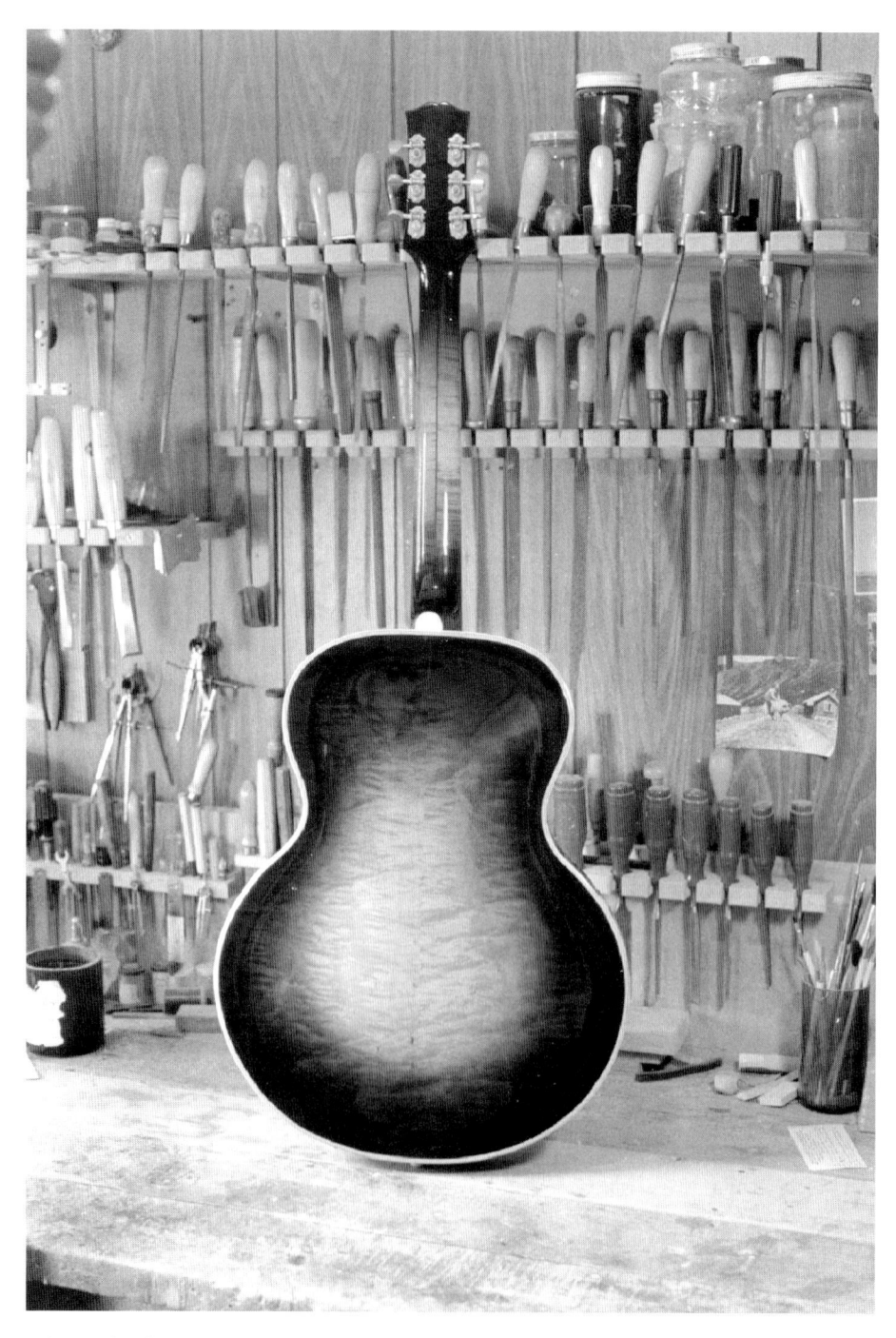

The back of D'Angelico #1002. *(Photo courtesy of John Monteleone Archive.)*

Back of the headpiece of D'Angelico #1002. *(Photo courtesy of John Monteleone Archive.)*

with that idiom. Strictly speaking, however, there is no such thing as a "jazz" guitar; there are merely instruments that have certain musical characteristics, which individuals feel are appropriate for their chosen form of expression.

D'Angelico produced guitars as described above, gradually incorporating different designs and features as his prowess as an artist ripened. His first instruments bore no model names, but by 1934 he had established model designations. Although his instruments are referred to by these designations, they are not as descriptive and normative as one might assume. There are so many subtle (and some not so subtle) variations and alterations that the model designations are actually more like guidelines than specific and accurate descriptives.

The fifteenth D'Angelico. A common early model with headpiece inlay. *(Photo courtesy of Stan Jay/Mandolin Bros.)*

MODELS

By 1936 the basic D'Angelico models were Styles A, A-1, and B, the Excel (spelled "Exel" on a very few of the earliest examples of this model), and the New Yorker. The earliest examples (the pre-1936 L-5-styled instruments) were 16¼-inch instruments (measured at the lower bout). The A, B, and Excel were typically 16⅜- to 17⅝-inch instruments and differed only in ornamentation. D'Angelico would perhaps use a more figured piece of wood

A very early Excel, circa 1934, #1097. Note spelling of model: Exel.
(Photo courtesy of Jonathan Kellerman.)

for a back or neck of the more costly Excel model than for a less expensive Style A, A-1, or B, but musically speaking there was no inherent difference.

D'Angelico did not seek absolute precision regarding the sizes of his instruments. Examples of any of the models, even from the same period, often differed in size. Some of this variation is due to the fact that D'Angelico utilized different molds, but the very process he followed for creating instruments made varying-sized instruments a natural by-product. D'Angelico left a gap of approximately ½ inch in the molds, and after the sides were bent and placed in the mold it was not uncommon for them to shrink a bit, depending upon the particular pieces of wood. Thus, any expectation of exactness in D'Angelico body sizes is awry.

The New Yorker was originally an 18-inch instrument (ofttimes larger) and remained so until D'Angelico created a 17-inch instrument with New Yorker cosmetic features in 1943 (see appendix for serial numbers). The New Yorker cosmetic package consisted of split block inlays, more layers of binding, and the distinctive New Yorker headstock inlay (patterned after the Empire State Building, which was completed circa 1930).

Again, it is important to note that there was nothing radically different structurally from model to model. Nuances in graduation of the top and back, bracing structure and placement, depth, neck width and shape, body size, and silhouette were numerous and the norm, according to the prospective use of the instrument and the desire of the customer. There are, however, some generalizations that may be helpful to note.

The instruments from the 1930s were quite similar to Gibsons, yet still possess the D'Angelico sound (typically a bit more balanced and with more smoothness and clarity). In the forties the cosmetics became a bit fancier—more binding and larger position markers—and the shoulders became more broad. Styles A and B were dropped (in that order) as demand for the Excel and New Yorker prevailed. In the fifties, with the popularity of cutaway electric guitars on the rise, the instruments were also built

A late-1930s D'Angelico New Yorker. *(Photo courtesy of Gruhn Guitars.)*

This 1937 D'Angelico New Yorker (#1242) was originally sunburst and later refinished by D'Angelico to its present natural finish. *(Photo courtesy of Mark Cleary.)*

The original owner of this 1937 New Yorker (Robert Lessey) played with Fletcher Henderson. Note the etchings on the pickguard and inlay. *(Photo courtesy of Mark Cleary.)*

a bit "tighter" so as to impede the feedback effect. Throughout the fifties until his death in 1964, D'Angelico continued to dress up the instruments with larger headpieces, more binding, and more pearl (though one would hardly call the New Yorkers from the thirties plain).

There was no distinction made between carved models with built-in pickups and those with floating pickups, although they were constructed according to purpose. Typically the built-in instruments were a bit heavier and possessed straight or parallel braces (as opposed to the X-brace design, which D'Angelico also employed). D'Aquisto explained:

> When the pickup got more popular, the players would order the electrics, so John made carved instruments and cut holes in the top for the pickups. He made one for Chuck Wayne in the fifties when he was playing with George Shearing, all padded inside with green felt pool cloth which was glued right onto the wood so it wouldn't feed back, even covering the f-holes.

D'Angelico also made cutaway and noncutaway arch-top guitars with a single round or oval sound hole, the majority of which were completed in the forties. He even put his name on some plywood-bodied guitars. These instruments consisted of necks D'Angelico fashioned from solid wood, joined to plywood bodies made by Code (pronounced "Koday") and United Guitars, both from New Jersey. United Guitars was owned by Frank Forcillo, one of the fellows who worked for D'Angelico in the early days of D'Angelico's shop.

The plywood instruments were not numbered nor recorded in the ledger, though often the body will bear a designation such as "G7." These identifications were from the United or Code factories, not from D'Angelico, which makes these instruments very difficult to date. Most of them were similar in appearance and function to the Gibson Company's ES-175 model guitar.

A very few D'Angelico guitars were small "semi-solid" instruments, somewhat resembling an enlarged Gibson Les Paul model

Johnny Smith's D'Angelico made in 1955. The D'Angelico ledgers list this instrument as an Excel "1000," #1963. At this time the Excel headpiece had the broken-scroll pediment design, while the New Yorker did not. *(Photo courtesy of D. Louie.)*

D'Angelico oval hole, #1805, made January 7, 1949, 18¾ inches at lower bout. Restored by R. Benedetto. *(Photo courtesy of Jonathan Kellerman.)*

guitar. However, there is no record or verifiable recollection of John D'Angelico ever having created a solid-body instrument or a flat-top instrument.

D'Angelico also created other instruments that did not bear serial numbers, unusual one-of-a-kind instruments such as a mandolin in the shape of a rifle and a guitar with a large hook or teardrop on one end of the lower bout. Obviously these were not created with alternative musical dimensions in mind, but rather to satisfy the request of a customer desiring an instrument for a novelty act. It is important to note that D'Angelico was not only an artist creating works to satisfy his emotional and aesthetic needs but also a working artisan guided by pragmatic experience and the circumstances of the times—this was his livelihood and he was willing to do (within limits) what the customer requested.

John D'Angelico fitting the top to a one-of-a-kind instrument with a fin on the lower bout, circa 1957. *(Photo courtesy of John Monteleone Archive.)*

D'Angelico New Yorker, #2129, made in 1961. *(Photo courtesy of Jonathan Kellerman.)*

To illuminate D'Angelico's (and D'Aquisto's) mandolin creations and perspectives, I include the following quote from professional mandolinist and vintage instrument dealer Lawrence B. Wexer:

> The carved mandolin is an American invention. The original Orville Gibson–carved instruments of the 1890s were Orville's application of violin construction techniques, adapted to the mandolin. The introduction of the Gibson Company's F-5 mandolin in 1922, with f-holes, tone bar bracing and elevated fingerboard was the next evolutionary step in mandolin construction.
>
> D'Angelico began making mandolins while still a boy, working in his uncle's shop. These were Neapolitan-style, bowl-back instruments, made in the Italian-American tradition prevalent in early-twentieth-century New York. D'Angelico's creations show a typical Italian style of workmanship, in the way that Guarneri and other great Italian artisans exhibit a freedom and lack of rigidity in their realization of a musical instrument. The minor differences in body size, neck shape and asymmetry in body shape are an expression of this aesthetic. Since there were far fewer mandolins made than guitars, with most custom orders, it seems that the models were less well defined.
>
> There were a few basic model guidelines, partially based on price and features, but each mandolin seems a bit different in some way than all the others. The logbook [see appendix] shows three basic grades: Plain, Good, and Scroll. The Plain style usually refers to a teardrop-shaped, sunburst-finish mandolin with a plain, solid headstock and fingerboard flush with the top, similar in style to the Gibson Company's A-50 mandolin. These simpler models also featured dot fingerboard inlays, an unbound fingerboard, single-ply binding on the body, generic nickel strip tuners, generic clamshell tailpieces (smooth or scalloped), and f-holes. The Good style has a bit more binding on the body, an elevated fingerboard and fancier woods, often featuring block inlays in the fingerboard, and sometimes finished in blonde. The Scroll style can be interpreted as the deluxe model, "scroll" referring to the violin headstock in the

A plain D'Angelico from 1940 (#138). *(Photo courtesy of George Gruhn.)*

A D'Angelico mandolin (#114). *(Photo courtesy of Stan Jay/Mandolin Bros.)*

style of the Lyon & Healy Style A mandolin, or the body style, similar to the Gibson Company's F-5 mandolin. The fancier D'Angelico mandolins all show some combination of the following ideas: Lyon & Healy–inspired asymmetrical two-point body shape and violin scroll headstock or D'Angelico guitar-style headstock (broken-scroll pediment), f-holes, tone bar bracing, elevated fingerboard, and suspended pickguard.

In the way that D'Angelico's early guitars were influenced by the Gibson L-5, his mandolins show an influence of the Gibson F-5 in their internal construction. That instrument and the previously mentioned Lyon & Healy Style A mandolin were the major influences on D'Angelico's mandolin creations. As

A D'Angelico scroll-head mandolin (#112). *(Photo courtesy of George Gruhn.)*

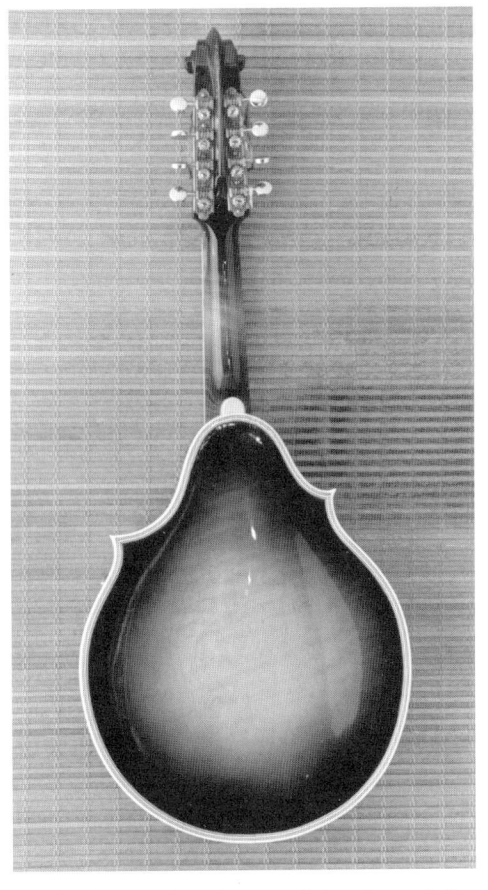

Back of the D'Angelico scroll-head mandolin (#112). *(Photo courtesy of George Gruhn.)*

An unusual scroll-body D'Angelico mandolin, circa 1950s. *(Photo courtesy of George Gruhn.)*

might be expected, another clear influence on D'Angelico's mandolins were his own guitars. D'Angelico's heavier top carving and large tone bars show that he had his own ideas about the carving of arched-top instruments in general.

In conversations with Jimmy D'Aquisto, he stressed that bluegrass music [a common venue for the mandolin] was not a factor in their concept of what a mandolin should sound like. He spoke of a Mr. Vicari, who played Paganini caprices and romantic Italian repertoire on a D'Angelico mandolin. This was "real" mandolin playing! The bright, bell-like sound and quick response of the Lyon & Healy mandolins was (and still is) considered the ideal by many classical and European-style mandolin players. John and Jimmy both agreed that this was the sound

THE INSTRUMENTS   **49**

A D'Angelico two-point mandolin, heavily influenced by D'Angelico's guitar designs; note the headpiece and fingerboard. *(Photo courtesy of Stan Jay/Mandolin Bros.)*

Detail of the D'Angelico two-point mandolin. *(Photo courtesy of Stan Jay/Mandolin Bros.)*

they were aiming for. The violin approach to playing mandolin, with the added use of tremolo and rapid single-note technique, framed both of these makers', concept of the mandolin.

D'Aquisto made only three mandolins, all in the early 1970s, though at the time of his death he had intentions of making a few modernistic mandolins, and there remained a few bent sides and sketched outlines on wood that give evidence of this. In the way that D'Angelico's mandolins were influenced by his own guitar-building, D'Aquisto's ideas about the mandolin stem from his work with D'Angelico and from his own unique concepts—the distinctive headstock design, ebony tailpiece, and exaggerated two-point body all show Jimmy's individual approach to building a mandolin. If D'Aquisto had completed at least one instrument during his later period it would have shown the same adventurous spirit we see in his modernistic guitars like the Solo or Avant Garde.

The violins he created have escaped my research; I was unable to locate one verifiable source or instrument.

Two ledger books log D'Angelico's works (see appendix). The first organized documentation of D'Angelico's instruments began with the first book, dated January 1936. Prior to 1936, the extant documentation, which is sorely incomplete, depicts serial numbers (starting with 1000) on two sides of a piece of paper, logged without rhyme or reason, with nonconsecutive serial numbers and dates, and some dates missing. This piece of paper is torn in fourths (where it had previously been folded) and exhibits signs of serious deterioration.

From 1936 until 1961 the ledgers were clearly written in both D'Angelico's hand and DiSerio's hand, though the majority of the entries appear to be DiSerio's writing. The format depicted the serial number, model, customer name, and date but did not indicate the color of the instrument (sunburst or blonde). Often the instruments were recorded several at a time, without regard for scholarly accuracy. The last entry of an instrument dated in the second book is Number 2123 (January 10, 1961), shortly after which D'Angelico reverted to the often-dateless "piece-of-

D'Angelico's shop as it looked from the street in the 1950s. Note the photos of D'Angelico players covering the wall—Victorian style. *(Photo courtesy of John Monteleone Archive.)*

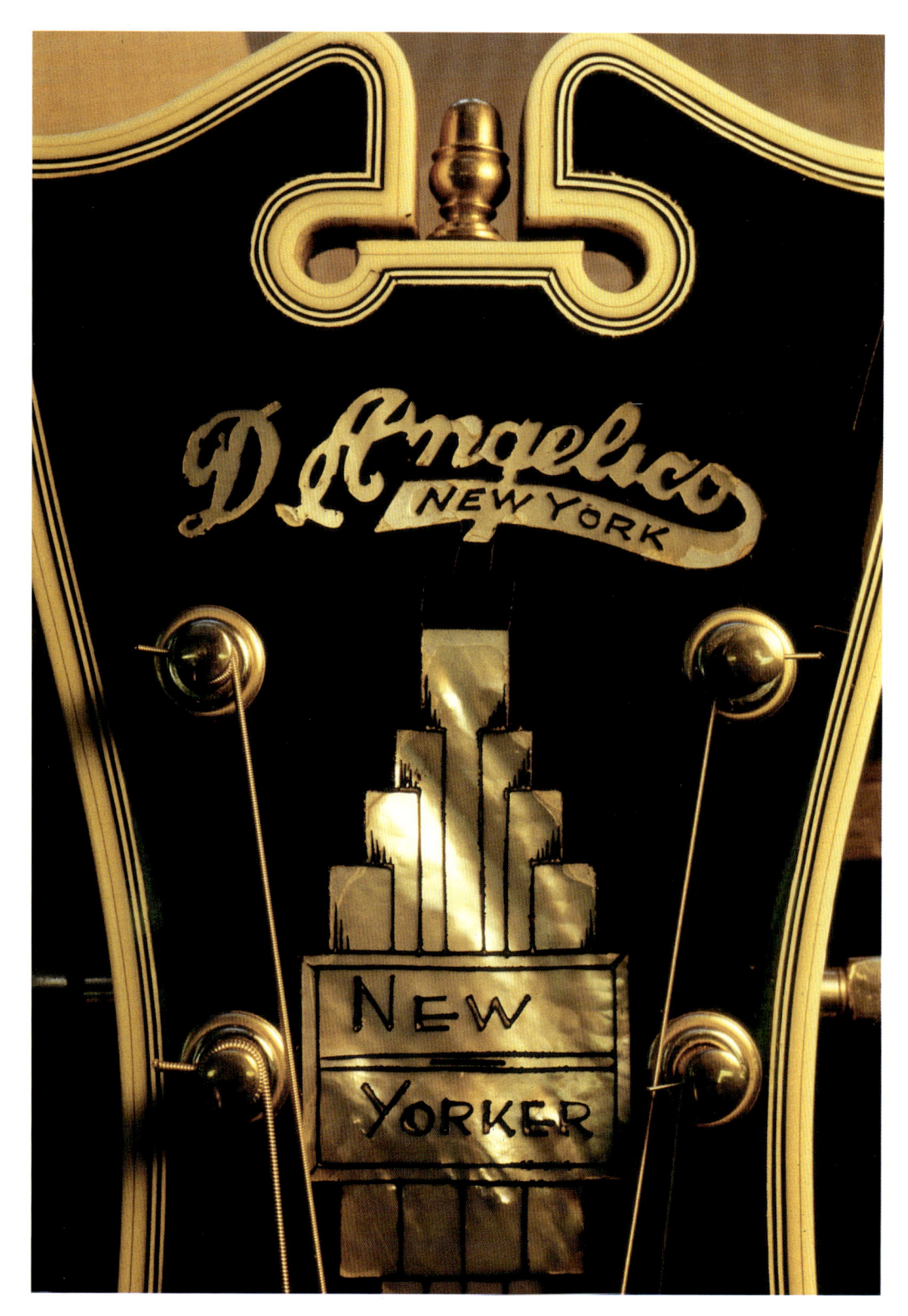

An extreme closeup of a D'Angelico New Yorker. *(Photo courtesy of John Monteleone Archive.)*

A moment profound in its ordinariness. Wood-dust flying, sweat forming, concentration severe: John D'Angelico carving an instrument circa 1957. *(Photo courtesy of John Monteleone Archive.)*

A D'Angelico family—a 1932 ukulele, a 1945 Excel, and a 1946 New Yorker. *(Photo copyright 1997 David C. Smith/Infinite Images; in the collection of the American Guitar Museum, New Hyde Park, NY; photo courtesy of Chris Ambadjes.)*

A D'Angelico New Yorker from 1946 (#1646). (Photo copyright 1997 David C. Smith/Infinite Images; in the collection of the American Guitar Museum, New Hyde Park, NY; photo courtesy of Chris Ambadjes.)

Back of the 1946 D'Angelico New Yorker. (Photo copyright 1997 David C. Smith/Infinite Images; in the collection of the American Guitar Museum, New Hyde Park, NY; photo courtesy of Chris Ambadjes.)

Body detail of the 1946 D'Angelico New Yorker. *(Photo copyright 1997 David C. Smith/Infinite Images; in the collection of the American Guitar Museum, New Hyde Park, NY; photo courtesy of Chris Ambadjes.)*

Headpiece detail of the 1946 D'Angelico New Yorker. *(Photo copyright 1997 David C. Smith/Infinite Images; in the collection of the American Guitar Museum, New Hyde Park, NY; photo courtesy of Chris Ambadjes.)*

Benny Mortel's 1945 D'Angelico Excel (#1592); atypical but original finish. This instrument appears in the wedding scene of the first Godfather film and was featured extensively on the film's soundtrack. (Photo copyright 1997 David C. Smith/Infinite Images; in the collection of the American Guitar Museum, New Hyde Park, NY; photo courtesy of Chris Ambadjes.)

Headpiece detail of Benny Mortel's 1945 D'Angelico Excel. (Photo copyright 1997 David C. Smith/Infinite Images; in the collection of the American Guitar Museum, New Hyde Park, NY; photo courtesy of Chris Ambadjes.)

Headpiece (left) and detail (right) of the 1932 D'Angelico ukulele commissioned by jazz great Benny Mortel. *(Both photos copyright 1997 David C. Smith/Infinite Images; in the collection of the American Guitar Museum, New Hyde Park, NY; photo courtesy of Chris Ambadjes.)*

A 1932 D'Angelico ukulele commissioned by jazz great Benny Mortel for his future wife; quite likely the first blonde D'Angelico instrument. *(Photo copyright 1997 David C. Smith/Infinite Images; in the collection of the American Guitar Museum, New Hyde Park, NY; photo courtesy of Chris Ambadjes.)*

A left-handed Excel from the 1950s with a D'Aquisto neck. The proverbial working musician's guitar, this instrument was used by Wayne Wright to accompany an array of musicians ranging in style from Judy Garland to Jimmy Page. (Photo copyright 1997 David C. Smith/Infinite Images; in the collection of the American Guitar Museum, New Hyde Park, NY; photo courtesy of Chris Ambadjes.)

Bearing testament to D'Angelico's willingness to experiment, this instrument was built for Tommy Lucas (guitarist in the pit orchestra of the *Ed Sullivan Show* for more than a decade). It was a commercial cello body fitted with a D'Angelico neck, fingerboard, and tailpiece. (*Photo copyright 1997 David C. Smith/Infinite Images; in the collection of the American Guitar Museum, New Hyde Park, NY; photo courtesy of Chris Ambadjes.*)

Headpiece detail of early 1930s instrument made for Harry Volpe.

From the earliest days of D'Angelico's career, when the name Harry Volpe was more well known than John D'Angelico, D'Angelico gave Volpe's name "headpiece prominence" on this early 1930s instrument made for Volpe. *(Photos courtesy of Jerry Haussler.)*

A late 1930s D'Angelico Excel with an unusually shaped pickguard and an added DeArmond pickup. *(Photos by Jerry Haussler.)*

Detail of the late 1930s D'Angelico Excel.

From left to right: John D'Angelico, customer Pete Girardi, and Vincent DiSerio at 2:34 P.M. in 1957. *(Photo courtesy of John Monteleone Archive.)*

John D'Angelico working on a soon-to-be New Yorker in the late 1950s. *(Photo courtesy of John Monteleone Archive.)*

A 1960 D'Angelico Excel (#2105). *(Photo by Robert Desmond and courtesy of the Guild of American Luthiers; special thanks to the Bob Mattingly Memorial Fund.)*

Headpiece detail of a D'Angelico New Yorker from 1960 (#2109). *(Photo by Jose Gaytan/Jim Whitaker; courtesy of Perry Beekman.)*

A D'Angelico New Yorker from 1960 (#2109). *(Photo by Jose Gaytan/Jim Whitaker; courtesy of Perry Beekman.)*

Back of the 1960 New Yorker (#2109). *(Photo by Jose Gaytan/Jim Whitaker; courtesy of Perry Beekman.)*

THE INSTRUMENTS **51**

D'Aquisto's two-point mandolin (#103) from 1972 (his last ledgered mandolin). *(Photo courtesy of George Gruhn.)*

D'Aquisto with one of his few mandolins. *(Photo courtesy of the author's archive.)*

Early D'Angelico ledger (in D'Angelico's hand.) *(Photo courtesy of James D'Aquisto and the author's archive.)*

THE INSTRUMENTS **53**

D'Angelico's ledger (in DiSerio's hand). Note the cutaway Excel made for Oscar Moore (#1793). *(Photo courtesy of James D'Aquisto and the author's archive.)*

paper method"—not unlike his manner of documentation at the beginning of his career. These books form a catalog of his carved guitars and some mandolins. There is no written record of the other instruments D'Angelico created, such as violins, plywood-bodied electrics, and novelty instruments.

WOODS

D'Angelico was quite consistent in the types of woods he utilized: spruce for the top; maple for the back, sides, and neck; and ebony for the fingerboard. This is not without exception, as there is at least one example of an instrument with mahogany back, sides, and neck; but the maple/spruce/ebony combination was status quo. The use of these woods for arch-top instrument designs goes back to seventeenth-century Italy, when violin makers such as the celebrated Amati family discovered that this combination of woods produced a superior result aurally, functionally, and visually.

Throughout most of his working life D'Angelico obtained wood from the specialty lumberyards in New York. These lumberyards were the primary suppliers for furniture makers, and received wood from Connecticut, Massachusetts, New York, Vermont, Georgia, Canada, and Madagascar. The ebony and Sitka spruce were imported, while the majority of the maple was domestic. During the fifties, when one of his customers requested imported wood, D'Angelico and the customer went together to a local wood-import company (owned by a Mr. Heiner, a friend of D'Angelico) to pick out the maple and spruce. From the mid-1950s until his death, D'Angelico used both imported and domestic maple, depending upon the situation, availability, and desire of the customer, though imported maple became more prominent in instruments made at the 37 Kenmare Street shop (1960–64). The maple was obtained in twelve-by-fifteen-foot lengths, nine or ten inches wide, one-and-one-half inches thick. As the wood was cut, D'Angelico searched for the curly or flamed pieces that he matched for the back—all done by look and feel.

The second numbered D'Angelico (on right) and the last numbered D'Angelico (on left, #1164) as they stand in the shop of luthier John Monteleone. *(Photo courtesy of John Monteleone Archive.)*

Though there is the notion that an instrument with figured wood is superior to one with less visual excitement, there is no inherent musical advantage of one over the other. Indeed, the figure or beauty of the wood is not related to the quality of an instrument's tone or durability nor to any other consideration than the visual. A plainly figured piece of wood may be every bit as acoustically responsive as a highly figured one, perhaps more so. Strictly speaking, the figure is an imperfection or scar in the wood, but of course it is not considered a flaw in the instrument.

NECKS

The widths, shapes, and thicknesses of necks on D'Angelico instruments vary greatly, as they were created for diverse playing styles and hand sizes. The first instruments from the early thirties had three-piece necks, as did the Lloyd Loar Gibson L-5s. As D'Angelico began incorporating his own ideas he switched to two-piece and then one-piece necks, depending upon the availability of woods and how he felt. He came to believe that there was no structural advantage in using a certain style of neck; thus, all styles being equal functionally, a one-piece neck was simply easier to fashion than a two-piece neck, and when the wood was available he did so.

All of the necks were originally reinforced by a nonadjustable system consisting first of a T-bar and then a tubular bar of cold-rolled steel. Later, when the Gibson Company's patent on the adjustable truss rod ran out, D'Angelico made it a standard feature on most of his instruments, from the late forties and onward. The adjustable truss rod worked on a principle similar to the Gibson Company's version, but just the opposite: Gibson had a reverse bow, rounded at the center and bowed back at either end; D'Angelico had a center bow, cupped at the center. Instruments with adjustable truss rods are simple to distinguish by the presence of a decorative removable truss rod cover at the headpiece just above the nut, typically fashioned from pearl or aluminum.

D'Angelico also created necks for players of other instruments, thus it is possible to find a Gibson, Epiphone, or other instrument with a D'Angelico neck and headpiece.

An extended fingerboard on a 1949 D'Angelico New Yorker. It is not uncommon to find this feature on a D'Angelico. *(Photo courtesy of Mark Cleary.)*

BRACINGS, LININGS, AND STAMPS

D'Angelico's carved tops were braced with spruce. The favored configuration from the early 1930s to the mid-1940s was the parallel or straight brace, and from then on the X-bracing pattern became more the norm—but not exclusively so. There are numerous examples of pre-1940s instruments with X-bracing, and 1950s instruments with the parallel bracing pattern. Bracing was done according to the role the instrument was intended to play for a particular customer.

An inside view of an X-braced D'Angelico Excel from the mid-1950s. *(Photo courtesy of Michael Katz.)*

The linings were normally fashioned from bass wood, a plain, light, strong wood that is almost white in color and readily absorbs glue. D'Angelico did not sign his instruments, but rather stamped them with his name and the serial number. However, some very early instruments bear signs of some type of writing on the inside back of the instrument. The numbered instruments began at 1000, the first instrument bearing the number 1001 (see appendix).

GRADUATION OF TOPS AND BACKS

The tops and backs of the D'Angelico guitars were finely graduated and were tested during carving by tapping and flexing, as well as by measurement with a gauge to ensure consistency. They were rather thick and were carved in the tradition of the famed violin makers of seventeenth-century Cremona, Italy—thicker in the center and thinner at the edges. This characteristic is generally accepted as the paramount arch-top carving principle in obtaining balance, sustain, and resonance.

Graduating tops and backs is an extremely complex procedure. The rigidity of the wood (which varies vastly even among pieces of equal thickness), the desired curve or arch, the dimensions, the prospective bracing pattern, the role the instrument is expected to perform for the prospective player—all need to be taken into account when performing this important aspect of creating a carved-top instrument. In keeping with the Amati/Stradivari tradition, D'Angelico did not seek absolute precision in the working of the thicknesses, as art and science are not always confluent.

CUTAWAY

The cutaway design became popular and prominent in the 1940s. The Gibson Company introduced the cutaway on arch-top guitars in 1939 and termed it "Premier." Soon many players realized

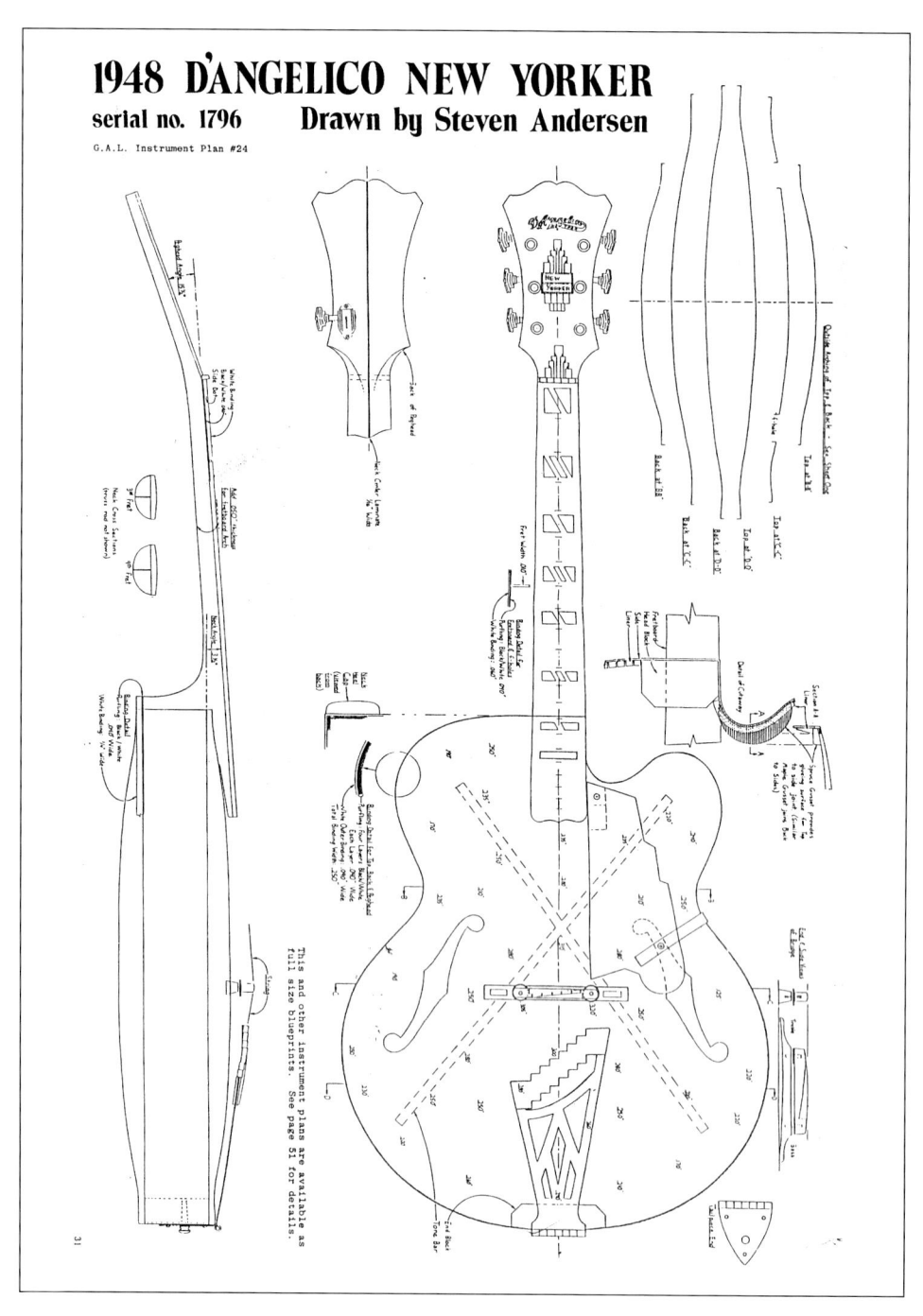

A drawing by luthier Steven Andersen of a 1948 D'Angelico New Yorker, noting all the measurements and thicknesses. *(Courtesy of the Guild of American Luthiers.)*

John D'Angelico showing a customer the early stages of the customer's New Yorker in the 1950s. *(Photo courtesy of Ray Gogarty.)*

the usefulness of having access to the upper frets, an option that was becoming increasingly interesting as the role of the guitar was expanding to that of a solo or "single-line" instrument, not unlike the saxophone or trumpet.

D'Aquisto noted, "In the beginning John thought the cutaway would be more of a problem, the bending of the wood and all, but he eventually embraced the design." The ledger books show the first cutaway made by D'Angelico was an Excel model made in 1947. "He thought the guitar would lose sound with the cutaway, which does happen, but he didn't feel it was an inferior design," D'Aquisto added.

Acoustically, the cutaway does alter the sound, but the alteration is in many cases negligible if not inaudible. D'Angelico carved the tops of his instruments before the cutaway portion of the instrument was cut away. There are subtle differences in the shapes and depths of the cutaways on D'Angelico guitars. As noted previously regarding the carving of the tops and backs, D'Angelico was not seeking orthodoxy in his artistry. Experimentation and alteration were constants in his process, and they became incarnate in all of the details of his work throughout his whole life of lutherie.

FINISHES

All of D'Angelico's first guitars featured a sunburst finish—a method of coloring in which dark shading at the outer edges of an instrument becomes gradually lighter towards the center (as the early Gibson L-5 was shaded). D'Angelico eventually began trying various colors, such as red sunburst (red to yellow), cherry to yellow, dark brown to yellow, red to pink, solid black, solid red, solid white, and a natural or blonde finish—whatever a customer might desire (within reason). The sunbursts were smaller in the thirties and gradually became more open and soft as D'Angelico experimented with the process.

The finish of an instrument is not unlike the binding, in that it serves both to protect and beautify the instrument. It is interesting to note that an acoustic instrument would actually sound its best without any finish whatsoever, but it would be completely unprotected and highly vulnerable to environmental changes, thus making it impractical.

D'Angelico's first method of shading involved applying the color directly to the wood and then completing the process with clear lacquer. By the mid-1940s the procedure for lacquer application was as follows: several coats of clear lacquer went onto the instrument first, followed by the shading process, and then several more coats of clear lacquer sealed the shading and completed the process. Once the final coats of clear lacquer had dried, the instrument was lightly sanded and then buffed to a mirror-like finish. That buffing was done by hand until the mid-1950s, at which time D'Angelico purchased a buffing machine.

INLAY AND BINDINGS

As might be expected, the inlay work on D'Angelicos varies greatly, especially on those instruments made in the thirties. The headstock inlays on the very early instruments feature a mother-of-pearl banner with "D'Angelico" etched into its center, as well as some sort of decorative design beneath it, also in mother-of-pearl. The Louis Handel Company, just around the corner from the D'Angelico shop, put the D'Angelico name into the headpieces. Joseph Schaffner (the engraver who also made and engraved the D'Angelico tailpieces) did the custom engraving in the pearl inlays in the headpiece, as well as any custom etching on the fingerboard inlays and pickguard.

Headpiece of a mid-1930s New Yorker (#1242). Note the inlay and etchings. *(Photo courtesy of Mark Cleary.)*

Common features for models Style A, Style B, and Excel included block inlays on the fingerboard (sometimes etched) and some sort of headpiece inlay displaying the model name. Of course, there are more than a few exceptions to that norm, as one can note from the earliest D'Angelico promotional flyer, which depicts pearl dot markers on the model Style A. The New Yorker inlay is typified by the split block inlays on the fingerboard, as well as the distinctive headstock inlay. As D'Aquisto explained it, "The step design for the headpiece was taken from the Empire State Building. It was designed by a jewelry designer friend of John's named Duke, who also made the templates John used for the split block fingerboard inlays."

There are many beautiful variations of inlay patterns—custom etchings of suns and flowers in the block inlays, stairstep pearl inlays on the bridge, etchings outlining the pickguard and split block fingerboard inlays—all in keeping with the individuality of his instruments, and one of the features that make these instruments so intriguing.

The binding material around the body, f-holes, fingerboard, and headpiece was made of nitrate celluloid, the same material from which the early cinema films were made. Binding was used both to protect the instrument and to beautify it by providing a contrast to the wood, which was especially effective on sunburst instruments.

D'Angelico purchased his binding material from a small shop on Broadway in sheets, which he cut to the desired thicknesses in his shop. As with the inlay, the binding configurations varied greatly, especially in the earlier years. As one might guess, the less-expensive models had simpler bindings, whereas the Excel and New Yorker had more elaborate designs. The bindings became thicker and fancier in the 1950s and 1960s as D'Angelico saw the guitar playing a more prominent role in music. His understanding of visual prominence manifested itself with increased layers of binding, more pearl, and larger headpieces.

The headpiece design was originally similar to the Gibson Company's L-5, but D'Angelico soon incorporated a broken-scroll pediment design that framed an ornamental cupola. The design dates back at least to the first century B.C.; a similar design was noted in Roman architecture at Petra, a rich oasis between Arabia and the Mediterranean. However, it is unlikely that first-century Roman architecture was the direct impetus for D'Angelico's design, as this type of design has been used in many contexts and formats since the first century.

In both binding and inlay, there are a number of examples of work that might be viewed as a bit sloppy. Some might view these instruments as inferior, yet as is the case with the figure of the wood, such irregularities do not impede the performance of the instrument as a musical tool. Those pedantic enough to judge an instrument by cosmetic imperfections miss the essence of D'Angelicos entirely. The magnitude of the creative/refinement successes inherent in D'Angelico instruments leave cosmetically technical considerations wanting. The parts of any artistic composition—a painting, a piece of music, a story, or a musical instrument—are not meant to be judged separately but by how they affect the whole. Another perspective might understand these imperfections as part of the charm and character, which actually make the instruments more interesting and human.

One unfortunate note about the D'Angelico bindings from the 1950s is that many instruments from this period were bound with material that was defective. Surely the defect was imperceptible at the time D'Angelico purchased and applied the material; but nonetheless, a number of instruments from that decade have bindings (and pickguards, which were fashioned from the same material) that are now deteriorating.

TAILPIECES

The first tailpieces were made of steel by the original Grover Company. They were quite plain and were plated with either chrome or nickel. After a very short while they began to bear the D'Angelico name and were being fashioned from brass and then gold-plated (though the simpler models were often fitted with tailpieces that were not gold-plated).

The tailpieces made expressly for D'Angelico were made by the Joseph Schaffner Company on Crosby Street in lower Manhattan. As mentioned before, it was Mr. Schaffner who engraved the D'Angelico name into the tailpiece—first by hand, and in later years by machine. The tailpiece was one of the few items, along with the name "D'Angelico," inlaid in mother-of-pearl, and the tuners, that was not made in D'Angelico's shop.

The familiar stairstep tailpiece was introduced in the late thirties and went through alterations of shape, thickness, weight, and ornamentation throughout D'Angelico's career. The stairstep design was created for musical reasons of equal string tensioning (a concept with which D'Aquisto disagreed). It is quite common to find earlier instruments with the stairstep tailpiece affixed, due

Bridge and tailpiece of an early 1950s New Yorker. Note that the treble side of the bridge is longer at the base. *(Photo courtesy of Mark Cleary.)*

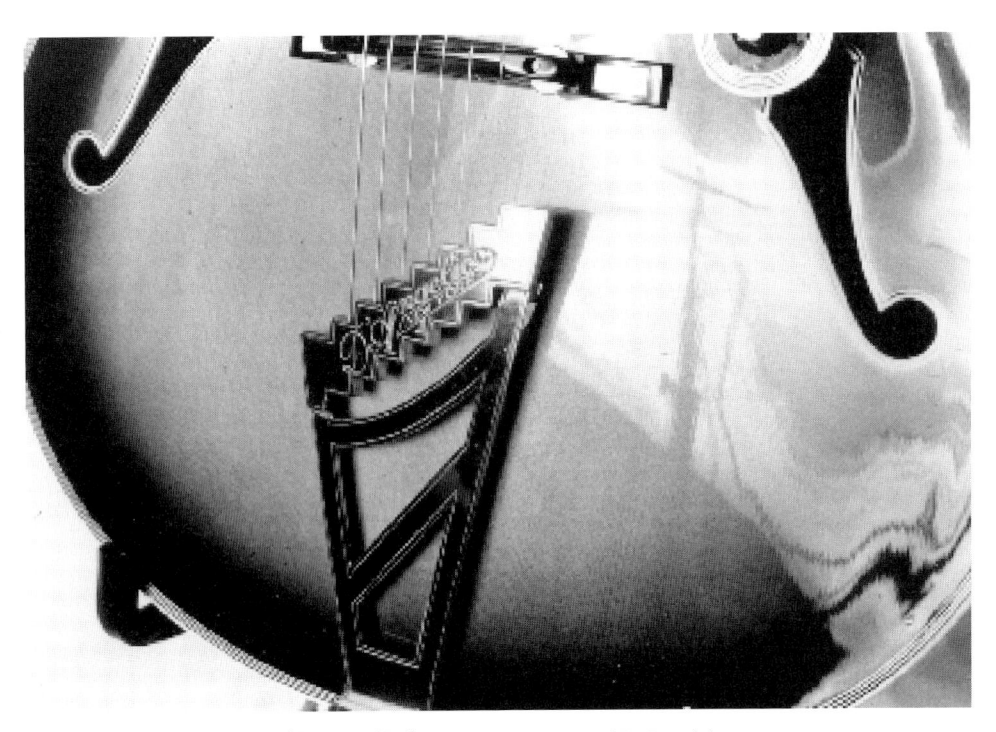

Tailpiece of Johnny Smith's New Yorker. *(Photo courtesy of D. Louck.)*

A 1936 D'Angelico New Yorker. Note the star-engraved tailpiece and the stair-step pearl-inlaid bridge. *(Photo courtesy of Mark Cleary.)*

to the fact that it was quite common for players to take their instruments back to D'Angelico's shop for adjustments and updating. Many found the stairstep tailpiece to be aesthetically stirring and requested D'Angelico to replace the original tailpiece with one of the new stairstep designs.

PICKUPS

D'Angelico was most concerned with building an acoustic instrument and did very little with pickups other than affix the style of pickup that the customer desired to an instrument. Pickups became popular in the late 1930s, the most common type being the DeArmond 1100, also known as the "Rhythm Chief" or FHC, made by Rowe Industries of single-coil design. Many players outfitted their D'Angelicos with these pickups, which sometimes required cutting into the pickguard.

As arch-top instruments fitted with pickups became more popular in the 1950s, some players desired to have instruments with pickups cut directly into the top of the guitar. Many of these instruments were sent to the Bigsby Company in California and equipped with Bigsby pickups, and at the customer's request, a Bigsby tailpiece. From D'Aquisto's point of view, "John didn't care at all about pickups and he didn't make a guitar designed for a pickup, he just made an acoustic guitar. For players that wanted an electric guitar, he braced and carved the instrument to accommodate the pickups."

This is not to imply that the instruments did not function brilliantly with a pickup, as many fine guitarists made extensive use of D'Angelico instruments equipped with some type of electronics. However, it is interesting to note that D'Angelico's intent was almost exclusively to create responsive acoustic instruments. Indeed, it was the acoustically responsive character of D'Angelico instruments that initially drew most players to them, notwithstanding the fact that these same players often utilized their guitars with pickups. Jazz guitarist Johnny Smith was one:

When I went down to pick up my D'Angelico I was not only in a tizzy to play it, but I had a job to do that night at a club. When John finally got it strung up I was so struck by the beauty of the sound that I couldn't be bothered with a pickup, and I didn't have the time to spare; so I took the guitar to the club where I was on the bill with George Shearing. I played the D'Angelico right into the microphone and it was wonderful. George's guitarist at the time was Toots Thielmans, and he was so impressed with the instrument that he put down his electric and used my D'Angelico the same way!

BRIDGES, TUNERS, AND TOOLS

The bridges for D'Angelico instruments were fashioned from solid pieces of ebony (or, very rarely, rosewood). D'Angelico created them in both adjustable and nonadjustable configurations. The earlier bridges were very thin, almost fragile; later they became thicker, with mother-of-pearl inlay on either side. D'Aquisto remembered the first time he saw D'Angelico's design for the angled bridge:

> I questioned it because Gibson had those steps and a big company like them had to know what was right. But as I got to know the instrument and the scale and all, I learned that the guitar is built on a tempered scale—it can never be perfectly tuned. By adding steps you are changing the harmonics, changing the scale length of each string. If you temper each string to be flat as it gets thicker, like a piano, the slight angle back to the low E-string [as D'Angelico's bridges were designed] is the truth.

The tuners utilized on D'Angelico instruments were made by either the Waverly Company or the Grover Company. Most common on D'Angelico instruments are the Grover Company's "Imperial"-style tuner, visually noteworthy for their stair-step design.

The tools with which D'Angelico worked were very ordinary—the same tools any hobbyist might have, such as a band saw, jigsaw, table saw, and buffing machine. The chisels he utilized for carving and detailing were made by the Berg Company from Sweden.

ADVERTISING

Of all the gifts D'Angelico possessed, business savvy was not one of them. His production was always small, but he traded being prolific for having a hand in each instrument he put his name to.

Unlike the major guitar manufacturers of the day, D'Angelico never had any sort of endorsement agreements with players. He did, however, make several attempts at promotion. There was one brochure or flyer with a photo of a noncutaway New Yorker with a few words extolling the then-new instrument's virtues. It was similar in style to the promotional materials disseminated by Gibson at that time and read a bit like an advertisement for a new automobile: "See how easily it handles!"

In the late 1930s a prominent New York guitarist named Anthony Antone did some promotional tours demonstrating D'Angelico's instruments. A typical letter follows:

> June 18, 1938
>
> New York City
>
> Dear Mr. Patire,
>
> During a tour throughout New Jersey I will be in your town for two or three days. Though we have never met, I wonder if you would be so kind as to send me the following information. Do you believe I can make the acquaintance of five or more guitarists while I am there?
>
> The reason for this is that I would like to show them some of the material I am taking along. This material includes the latest models in D'Angelico Guitars, Tenor Guitars, Mandolins, as well as Strings, Plectrums, etc.
>
> No one is under any obligation to buy anything I demonstrate since this tour is financed by the D'Angelico Co.
>
> If you co-operate with me upon my arrival, I will reciprocate

An early (circa 1935) promotional brochure for D'Angelico guitars. *(Courtesy of Al Valenti.)*

Reverse of the early (circa 1935) promotional brochure for D'Angelico guitars. (Courtesy of Al Valenti.)

by giving you a complete set of all my compositions, as well as some by Frank Victor and Harry Volpe. Besides this I will play these compositions, Eddie Lang's works, the most modern Rhythm and Single String Choruses, Runs, Fill-ins, etc. for you and other guitarists.

Since I will practically be a stranger there I would sincerely appreciate an immediate reply so that I can look forward to your co-operation and also let you know the exact date of my arrival.

Thanking you in advance,

I remain,

Musically yours,

Anthony Antone

The above request was granted and Mr. Joe Patire offered his barbershop for the demonstration of D'Angelico instruments by Antone in 1938.

Whenever D'Angelico advertised via a flyer, he included a list of players who utilized his instruments. In compiling that list, D'Angelico printed the names in the order in which they came to him, with no particular rhyme or reason. When one advertisement appeared, Anthony Antone's name was last. Antone was evidently not of the belief that one "saves the best until last." He became angry with D'Angelico and severed relations with the master luthier.

Most of the advertising for D'Angelico instruments was done by word of mouth or by players seeing their favorite guitarists playing a D'Angelico. Guitar instructor and guitar method book publisher Mel Bay may have been the greatest source of visibility for D'Angelico guitars, as Bay's guitar method books consistently featured photographs of Mr. Bay with his blonde D'Angelico New Yorker. To this day Mel Bay Publications prints guitar books depicting D'Angelico and D'Aquisto guitars gracing their covers.

The Experience of Generations of Guitar Makers is Reflected in this MASTERPIECE

THE INCOMPARABLE qualities of the D'Angelico guitars are the embodyment of generations of guitar making. The expert craftsmanship and tone qualities, are inherent qualities handed down to the present John D'Angelico. D'Angelico guitars so ably express the superior craftsmanship, that they have been compared to the Stradivarius. All D'Angelico guitars are hand-made. Only the finest woods are selected. The tops and backs are carved from 1¼ inch stock — hand graduated with the same degree of skill as are the instruments of the old masters. Musicians recognize this superior craftsmanship and many of the famous guitar virtuosos and orchestra players use D'Angelico guitars exclusively.

During years of making guitars for artists and leading guitar players, D'Angelico perfected a guitar which has all the features desired and an unmatched tone quality and volume. This guitar — the modern instrument of modern masters — is known as the D'Angelico NEW YORKER.

D'Angelico guitars have always retained a leading place as the choice of artists and masters. The crowning achievement in the field of guitars is the NEW YORKER.

Endorsed by Leading Musicians and Critics

The D'Angelico NEW YORKER

The D'Angelico NEW YORKER embodies every feature making it particularly sensitive, rich in tone, easy to play and easy to handle. It has:

- Grand Auditorium Size — 18 inches wide, 21 inches long.
- Selected curly maple back, sides and neck.
- Finest grained reddish brown spruce top shaded to golden sunburst in center of top, back and neck.
- Sound holes and edges bound with black and white Ivroid.
- Oval ebony finger board with modernistic inlaid position blocks.
- High content nickel silver frets — extra wide and oval.
- Neck reinforced with steel T Bars from 1st to fifteenth frets.
- High Ivroid bound, streamlined pick guard.
- Hand carved pearl inlaid adjustable ebony bridge.
- Modernistically designed, diagonally stepped tail piece. Gold plated.
- New Grover enclosed gear type non-slip pegs. Gold plated.
- Neck joins body at 14th fret.

This hand made masterpiece is the pride and joy of every guitar player. Comes with Deluxe Alligator grained case, lined with heavy silk plush. Fitted with latest type enclosed clasp hardware. *Price of D'Angelico* NEW YORKER *with case* $400

Used in Leading Orchestras. See other Side

D'Angelico promotional flier from the late 1930s. *(Photo courtesy of Al Valenti.)*

THE INSTRUMENTS 75

Announcing
The D'Angelico NEW YORKER

The Modern Masterpiece from the Experienced Hand of Generations of Guitar Makers

See—Hear and—Try THE D'Angelico NEW YORKER

To appreciate the skill and generations of guitar making craftsmanship embodied in the NEW YORKER, one must see it — listen to the deep resonant tones — and pluck the strings to see how easily it handles.

Call us or write us and we will be glad to give you an opportunity to try and hear the D'Angelico New Yorker. Besides this outstanding Masterpiece, John D'Angelico also makes a complete line of guitars and mandolins at various price levels.

JOHN D'ANGELICO
40 Kenmare Street
NEW YORK, N. Y.

Used by the MODERN MASTERS OF THE GUITAR

AL VALENTI
Referred to as a genius by authorities and critics. Famous for plectrum playing of classics composed and written for finger playing. Mr. Valenti uses D'Angelico guitars exclusively.

FAMOUS ORCHESTRA PLAYERS WHO HAVE CHOSEN D'Angelico GUITARS

AL VALENTI.................*with* JOE REICHMAN
BENNY MORTELL.............*with* JOHNNY GREEN'S OR.
TONY COLUCCI..............STAFF ARTIST, N.B.C.
CHICK ROBERTSON......*with* JOE VENUTI'S ORCHESTRA
ROC HILLMAN..........*with* JIMMY DORSEY'S ORCHESTRA
FRANK PARRISH.........*with* ABE LYMAN ORCHESTRA
ROBERT LESSEY................*with* DON REDMAN
JOEL LIVINGSTON...............*with* VAN ALEXANDER
JOE SINACORI...................*with* EDDIE DELANGE
JOHN TRUHART................*with* ELLA FITZGERALD
EDDIE ASHERMAN...............*with* XAVIER CUGAT
BOB REMINGTON........*with* THE KIDOODLERS, N.B.C.
DON ROMEO
 with TED STRAETER, FEFE'S MONTE CARLO ORCHESTRA
ANTHONY ANTONE....EMINENT GUITARIST, COMPOSER

D'Angelico promotional flier from the late 1930s. *(Photo courtesy of Al Valenti.)*

Promotional flier for "Vin Cente and Jovinelly." *(Photo courtesy of Vincent Valenti and the author's archive.)*

VIN CENTE and JOVINELLY
will play your favorites in the CRYSTAL BAR at

MARYLAND CLUB
MARLBORO PIKE   *Gardens*   HILLSIDE 0600

John D'Angelico left himself to the world in the form of his instruments. Each of D'Angelico's instruments bears testimony to some element of his personality, his character, his artistry, his soul. D'Angelico's life and works further manifested themselves in his protege, James D'Aquisto, thus blessing yet another generation of musicians and artists with refined musical tools and a beacon of artistry.

PART II

D'Aquisto

D'Aquisto Means "To Acquire"

D'Aquisto at work in the late 1970s. *(Photo courtesy of J. Olsen.)*

3
The Man

James L. D'Aquisto was born on November 9, 1935, in Brooklyn, New York. Both sets of his grandparents were originally from Palermo, Sicily, and came to this country in the early 1910s. D'Aquisto's mother, Mary (Maria), was born in Hoboken, New Jersey; his father, James (Vincent), was born in Brooklyn. They were united in marriage in 1933, and two years and two days later James, the first of two children, was born, to be joined six years later by a brother, Joseph.

As a boy D'Aquisto displayed a penchant for creating with his hands. His mother recalled:

> As a boy he did a lot of drawing—cartoon work. At Christmas he'd do murals. When he was just four or five he'd sit and make model airplanes—carve them and glue them together. He also used to work with clay and soft rubber; in fact, I have a head of his grandfather on the D'Aquisto side of the family made out of clay, and a head of an Indian made out of soft rubber that James carved when he was seven or eight. He was always doing something artistic.
>
> Both of my sons were loners like myself. They had loads of friends, but they liked their own company best. James didn't do much reading, but he was very productive with his hands. He liked to play with toys that had to be put together. One day when he was six, he was very sick with a fever of 103. I called the doctor, and when he arrived we found James at the kitchen table carving a model, all wrapped up in blankets.

D'Aquisto at fifteen months. *(Photo courtesy of Phyllis D'Aquisto.)*

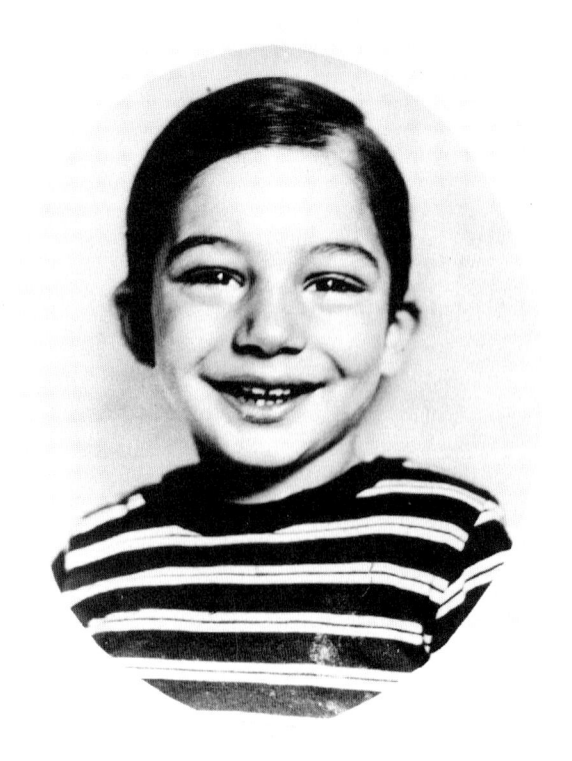

D'Aquisto at age 2. *(Photo courtesy of Phyllis D'Aquisto.)*

Along with his interest in creating things with his hands, D'Aquisto's boyhood was filled with music. The favored music at the D'Aquisto household was classical, heard via radio and live as well. Mary D'Aquisto continued:

> When he was very young he had a friend whose father was a doctor that loved opera, as my father did, so James and his friend would go to the opera and listen. I believe this was a basic and important influence in his young life. He always liked peaceful and melodic music, which was like his personality.

As D'Aquisto grew older, his musical interests expanded to incorporate jazz, as well as rhythm and blues. His first exposure to the guitar came from his family. The entire family would gather on weekends to socialize, feast, and share music. Their music was in the Italian family tradition, with guitar, mandolin, violin, and piano, as well as singing. The teenage D'Aquisto watched his father play the guitar and became intrigued enough to desire formal lessons.

D'Aquisto on the lap of his maternal grandfather in the late 1930s.
(Photo courtesy of Phyllis D'Aquisto.)

Before the guitar, however, another popular instrument of the day interested D'Aquisto:

> At first I took trumpet lessons. I took three lessons and then I thought, "I can't make this thing!" There was something about the guitar, it seemed like you could do so much more with it—chords, lines, everything. The modern jazz thing was starting to come in then with players like Jimmy Rainey, Tal Farlow, Jim Hall, and Joe Puma. I used to go to Basin Street, Birdland, and all those places. I became jazz insane!

D'Aquisto began taking lessons from Anthony Antone, the prominent New York guitarist who had had a falling-out with D'Angelico, and he began getting together with friends from his neighborhood who were equally interested in music. Mary D'Aquisto remembered his fascination with playing the guitar:

> In his early teens he formed a group with saxophones, guitars, and singing. The rest of the family would sit in the breakfast room with an old TV so they would have space to practice in the living room. You should have heard some of the things they came up with—heaven help us! They eventually got better, but I was just happy he was home. I'd wake up in the middle of the night and James would be recording some kind of nonsense on a tape recorder he had. He just liked to create, with his hands and with music.

In Frederick Cohen's award-winning film on D'Aquisto entitled *The New Yorker Special*, there is a short segment showing the teenage D'Aquisto playing music with his friends.

School held no particular interest for D'Aquisto. He first attended a parochial school that made no provision for hands-on courses; thus, the young D'Aquisto became bored with the subjects that had little to do with his interests. By the age of 16 he was attending a commercial art school, but he was soon invited to leave. The school informed his parents that he was merely wasting his time and that it would be best for all involved if he secured employment.

THE BELL HOPS

D'Aquisto with his musical group, The Bell Hops, circa 1960. *(Photo courtesy of Phyllis D'Aquisto.)*

D'Aquisto's first position in the work force was that of a "runner" at the New York Stock Exchange on Wall Street, a position which lasted a mere nine months, but which introduced D'Aquisto to some facets of the world that were new to him. His next position found him as a stock boy at the Lord & Taylor Department Store, a position he was to hold until meeting John D'Angelico at the ripe old age of 17.

As D'Aquisto worked in these positions, he continued his efforts with the guitar—his groups and the lessons with Antone. Antone, who had still not forgiven D'Angelico for the perceived slight in his advertisement, guided D'Aquisto to Frank Favilla to replace the Harmony Monterray guitar that D'Aquisto had been using. (That Favilla instrument was owned by D'Aquisto until his death. It was fitted with a D'Angelico neck after D'Aquisto began apprenticing at the D'Angelico shop.) D'Aquisto continued meeting more musicians and guitarists, one of whom introduced the young D'Aquisto to D'Angelico:

> This guy had a brand new Gibson L-4 with a "Rhythm Chief" pickup on it. He came to the house and introduced himself to me, and I'd never seen a guitar that looked as good as his L-4. This guy brought D'Angelico's name to me. He said, "Hey, you want to see the greatest guitars in the world, man, you've got to see a D'Angelico. Everybody that's the best plays a D'Angelico."
>
> So one day this new friend took me down to John's on a Saturday. John was finishing up an 18-inch New Yorker for Al Chenet; I think it was around 1953. I saw the guitar and I flipped. John said, "Would you like to try it?" So I sat down and he placed it in my lap; I played a chord and I couldn't believe it—it sounded like a piano. I'd never heard anything like that or ever thought a guitar was supposed to sound like that!

From that point onward, the D'Angelico shop held unprecedented interest for D'Aquisto. After his workday at Lord & Taylor, D'Aquisto would go to D'Angelico's shop and hang out. He would also take along gadgets that he'd made at home for the

D'Aquisto (far left, playing a Mosrite bass) performing in the late 1950s or early 1960s. *(Photo courtesy of Phyllis D'Aquisto.)*

guitars to show to D'Angelico—bridges, pickguards, and electric attachments. He expressed his enthusiasm by his presence and character, and D'Angelico took notice:

> One day I was down there and I said, "I could stay here the rest of my life." John said, "Oh no you can't." He was in one of his moods. But one day he called me and asked me to come down to the shop. He introduced me to Vincent DiSerio and then asked me if I'd like to come to work with them. Of course I said yes. Jimmy [Vincent DiSerio's nickname] asked me if I was sure this is what I wanted to do, and he teased me about my name—D'Aquisto means "to acquire." I told them I'd love to learn all about making guitars. So I started, and I was making $35 a week. I was like the runner: I'd go to the stores, pick up the tuners, go get the tailpieces from downtown, take the necks to the engraver, all that. I cleaned the windows, swept the floors, everything—we all did that. On Friday we put away the tools and cleaned the shop so when Monday came the place would be spotless.

D'Aquisto was ecstatic and his family was supportive, though his mother does recall being initially a bit concerned:

> I was a little uptight at first because I thought he was giving up something where he could earn a living, where he wouldn't have to worry so much, but we never stopped him. My husband convinced me that if this was what James wanted, then it was a good thing.
>
> I guess he got the genes from both my husband and myself. My husband was a tool and die maker, and I was a designer with flowers and crafts. His grandfather was a custom tailor, so I guess it made sense.
>
> I didn't meet John until several years after James got his position. If my son could be happy with Mr. D'Angelico then I could be happy with Mr. D'Angelico. John was an idol to him—like a second father. James was always coming home talking about all of the prominent players he'd been able to have lunch with, all excited.

Eventually D'Aquisto began learning the rough work of the D'Angelico process from DiSerio and sharing the work DiSerio had done earlier, before D'Aquisto's presence supplemented the D'Angelico shop. D'Aquisto was eager to learn and would always watch and ask questions of D'Angelico and DiSerio. He would work on something new whenever the opportunity presented itself:

> Almost every day around 1:00 P.M. John would go out. He was a gadget buyer, and downtown Manhattan had all these hardware stores and tool-making shops and machine shops—West Broadway, Houston Street, Centre Street—and John would often be gone for two or three hours. DiSerio and I both knew this, and the minute John walked out the door, DiSerio would take off his apron, show me what to do as I was eager to learn, and then he'd read the newspaper. The time would pass, and as we knew about what time John would return, we'd both go back to doing what we had been doing before he left. That was it, every day.

Throughout D'Aquisto's apprenticeship, D'Angelico was never dictatorial. D'Aquisto recalls D'Angelico's instruction as, "This is what I want done and this is how I do it. You do it any way you like, but it must turn out as good or better than what I did." Indeed, D'Aquisto did make improvements:

> When John made a pickguard, and you can see this on the old ones, he never made the steps uniform. I took it and made it so all the steps angled the same way. I made new templates and changed that. The same thing with the headpiece. The Excel headpiece was my template; the notch and design were John's idea, and the uniformity of the shape of the D'Angelico headpiece was mine. The same case with the f-holes: I was doing the binding so I made new templates for the f-holes.

It was during the mid-1950s that D'Aquisto met his wife-to-be, Phyllis Fezza. The two married on May 16, 1959, and moved to an apartment in Brooklyn, where their first two children, Paula and Lisa, were born.

Though the pay was low, D'Aquisto loved his life at the D'Angelico shop—the work, the family-like environment, and the top players dropping by to visit. It was this atmosphere that laid the groundwork for his life's work. D'Aquisto learned not only about guitar-making but also about life. He was able to see the life and work of a master artist and the childlike delight of players upon receiving their guitars—as well as the abusive attitudes of those who were insensitive to D'Angelico's efforts. Johnny Smith recalled:

> I would always make a point to visit John whenever I could, as I was so amazed at what he did, and I had so much respect and admiration for him. I remember seeing him out on the sidewalk in front of the little shop working on some child's roller skate, repairing something that had broken. As he worked on the roller skate we visited, and a top professional guitarist who happened to have a guitar on order happened to come by. He became irate with John because he saw him working on a roller

skate instead of his guitar. This guitarist didn't realize that as John's shop had no humidity control, there were days when he couldn't do certain things due to the weather. That guitarist didn't realize you cannot hurry this type of artistry.

Indeed, time is often hostile to results.

By the time the building at 40 Kenmare Street was condemned in 1959, D'Aquisto was doing a number of things on the guitars: shaping and binding the headpieces, pickguards, f-holes, and pearl inlays; hand finishing; and other decorative procedures. Thus, with the condemnation of the building, and with DiSerio and D'Angelico vowing to never interact again (forcing the business to close), the young apprentice luthier was thrown into a confusing time. D'Aquisto began working in nightclubs as a bassist and guitarist but loathed it. He contacted DiSerio for possible employment with the Favilla shop and was rejected. He finally persuaded D'Angelico to open a shop at 37 Kenmare Street and the two of them, with some assistance from some neighborhood men, moved the entire operation across the street into the new shop.

By early 1960 D'Angelico and D'Aquisto were again creating guitars. Out of necessity, D'Aquisto began doing work that DiSerio had never attempted on the instruments, such as carving tops and backs, shaping necks and fingerboards—almost every detail of the process, save creating an instrument on his own.

When D'Angelico died, D'Aquisto was broken. His great sense of loss was that of losing a family member, for even D'Aquisto's own family recognized D'Angelico as the second father he'd become to D'Aquisto. Mary D'Aquisto recalled:

> He was very sad when John died. James was with John more than he was with his own family. His life was changing from day to night; it wasn't all happy anymore after John died. When James took the whole business over it was a big responsibility, and he took it on with devotion. It took him some time to adjust to all of the new things he came upon in his new role, but he really wanted to keep up that reputation John had shown him.

Not only was a loved one taken in death, but D'Aquisto's loss also extended itself to the prosaic reality of earning a living:

> I was completely lost. I felt horrible—emotionally crushed—and I certainly had no idea about what to do to earn a living. Even when I was working all day for John, I was out playing bass in clubs until 3:00 A.M. to earn money to support my family [by 1964 D'Aquisto and his wife had moved to Long Island and had just experienced parenthood for the third time with the arrival of daughter Pamela]. Now, again, I had to go back to playing full-time. I hated every minute of it.

D'Angelico's surviving brother encouraged D'Aquisto to go ahead and work in the shop, as there were instruments to complete and repairs to do. After several weeks of mourning,

D'Aquisto in his own shop in the mid-1960s. *(Photo courtesy of Phyllis D'Aquisto.)*

D'Aquisto reappeared at 37 Kenmare Street and began to work on the guitars. Oddly enough, though there were guitars in various stages of creation, nobody wanted D'Aquisto to finish them. D'Aquisto found that "nobody wanted me to make a guitar. Nobody would even give me credit if I wanted to buy tuners, let alone order a guitar from me. 'What's a D'Aquisto? Who wants that?' That's what I got."

The D'Angelico family made it clear to D'Aquisto that John had wanted him to have the business and they offered him the business, the goodwill, and the right to call himself "successor to D'Angelico" for three thousand dollars. As D'Aquisto had no money and little experience or knowledge of purchasing and owning a business, he contacted a person who was a friend of John's—a fellow who frequented the shop, owned two D'Angelicos, and happened to be a lawyer. D'Aquisto explained the situation to the man, who then offered to help and even loan D'Aquisto the money to purchase the business from the D'Angelico family. D'Aquisto was ecstatic:

> I thought he was the greatest guy on earth. Now, for his investment, he wanted to see the books. John had a string business as well as the guitar-making. The strings were made for John, and we sold them with the D'Angelico name. This lawyer saw that the string business was grossing $35,000 a year and that I'd need help with all of the legal aspects. He said he'd loan me the money and be my partner. Like a fool, I agreed.

On the advice of the lawyer, the signed agreement stipulated that the lawyer owned the business and that D'Aquisto would not own anything until he paid back the loan, plus interest. The D'Angelico family stepped out of the picture, and D'Aquisto's partner (whom he preferred not to name) stepped in. D'Aquisto recalls being uncomfortable with the situation but felt he had little choice; he also believed his partner to be honest and kind for helping him out. With time, D'Aquisto's perception began to change.

D'Aquisto opened the shop with the assistance of a fellow who had played drums in one of the bands he played with in the nightclubs, and began doing repairs. D'Aquisto did not attempt to make any instruments because he "had a mental block because John wasn't there." There were still plenty of repairs, however. His business partner showed up once a week, checked the books, asked how things were going, and left. D'Aquisto began to realize he'd made an error:

> One day I stopped him and said, "What's going on here? We're partners and I can never make enough to pay you back! I pay you back and you tell me it's just the interest. All you do is check the books to see how much we've made. I feel like I'm working for you!" It ended up that every time he came through the door we were arguing.

Despite all of the business travails that afflicted D'Aquisto, his artistic desires continued to mature, and one year after D'Angelico's death D'Aquisto raised the courage to make a guitar:

> There had been a set of pre-bent sides sitting in the shop for a year—one that John had started before he died. I took the sides and completed the process, and the instrument that I made was an exact D'Angelico guitar; the only difference was that the inlay at the top of the headpiece read "D'Aquisto," and it bore no model name in the decorative pearl beneath my name.

Even though D'Aquisto had previously performed almost every procedure required to create a guitar, and those tasks that he had not performed he nonetheless understood, it was a milestone for the young luthier: the instrument turned out just as he'd desired. The studio players in New York saw the instrument and were surprised because they couldn't see any difference between this new instrument and the D'Angelicos. From that guitar, D'Aquisto slowly began to get some orders.

Artistically his work was very gratifying, but the business arrangement was manifesting itself in unsettling ways. D'Aquisto

New York guitarist Don DeMarco with the fourth D'Aquisto ever made (#1004). Note the similarities between a D'Angelico and this incarnation of a D'Aquisto.

was now making fervent attempts to pay off his partner so he could have the business to himself, and he offered the instrument he'd just created as partial payment on the debt. His partner deducted the cost of the wood, as it was owned by the "corporation," and he deducted the cost of D'Aquisto's time because D'Aquisto did the work on "corporation time." Thus, instead of deducting the full value of the instrument ($850—the same price D'Angelico had been charging for one of his New Yorkers at the time of his death) from D'Aquisto's debt, the deduction was next to nothing. D'Aquisto found this situation abusive. Instead of receiving the money for the instruments with which he was filling orders, he was earning only $150 a week.

In his attempt to rid himself of his partner, D'Aquisto made another significant error:

> I was so disgusted. I had to give him the repair money and the money from the guitars I made, and I could never get enough to pay him off and be rid of him. I said, "You take the string business and I'll take the guitar business." He said, "Are you sure?" and I told him I was. He took out a legal pad and began writing this up: "I, James D'Aquisto, give up the rights to the string business . . . ," which was ridiculous! Like a stupid fool I sign it. He still owns all of the machinery because it's part of the corporation, so all I have is nothing.

To make matters worse, another tragedy awaited D'Aquisto. The day after Christmas, 1965, D'Aquisto came to work at 37 Kenmare Street to find everything that had strings on it had been stolen—all of the D'Angelicos in for repair, and D'Aquisto's own fifth guitar, which he'd just completed. Neither a merry Christmas nor a happy New Year were in the offing for D'Aquisto: he'd signed away the string business, the "corporation" (i.e., his partner) owned all the machinery and wood, and all of the guitars were gone.

D'Aquisto then elected to leave the city and set up shop in Huntington, Long Island, where he continued to attempt to purchase the machinery from his partner. In abject disgust, D'Aquisto finally issued the ultimatum to his partner: either sell me the machinery or get it out of my shop. The next day a moving truck pulled up and seven men began moving everything out. Upon their departure all that remained were two chairs, a large bench, and D'Angelico's spray booth for applying lacquer and shading (fortunately, D'Aquisto was able to salvage D'Angelico's carving planes used to carve the tops and back of instruments).

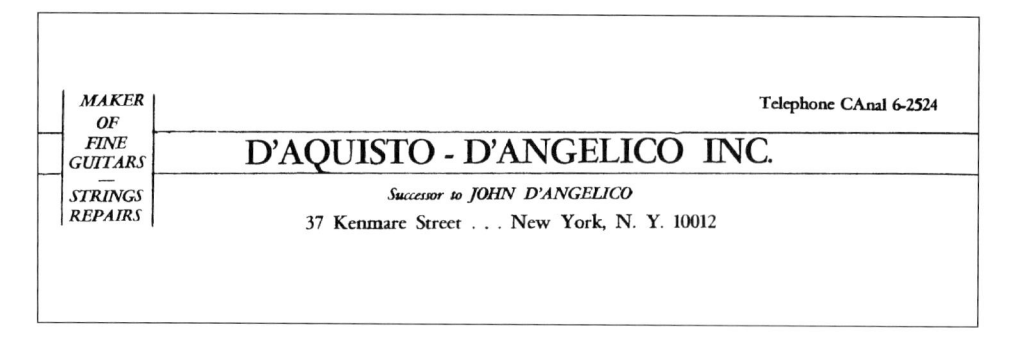

```
MAKER
  OF
 FINE         D'AQUISTO - D'ANGELICO  INC.          Telephone CAnal 6-2524
GUITARS
─────
STRINGS              Successor to JOHN D'ANGELICO
REPAIRS          37 Kenmare Street . . . New York, N. Y. 10012
```

D'Aquisto's letterhead shortly after D'Angelico's death. (*Courtesy of James D'Aquisto and the author's archive.*)

D'Aquisto recalls informing his ex-partner that the man hadn't acquired the D'Angelico name honorably and that he wouldn't live to enjoy it. Six months after the exodus of equipment from the 37 Kenmare shop, the man suffered a heart attack while driving his automobile, struck a pole, and was killed.

For the most part, D'Aquisto had next to nothing for the next three months, but he was determined to again create instruments:

> This was a terrible time. I went to the banks to get a loan and I couldn't get anything. I had no money, almost no tools, no string business, John was gone, and I had a wife and four kids to support [fourth daughter Jamie Lynn was born in 1965]. So, my brother made a bank loan for me which I paid off, and I bought the exact same machinery John had, right down to the Swedish chisels. The landlord at the shop was good enough to work with me while I got started up again, and my parents helped out the family with food and other necessities. I started to get a few orders.

The ten instruments D'Aquisto had created at the 37 Kenmare Street shop were starting to be seen by players around the city, and he began to get orders from some of the younger players. Few of the older players ordered instruments, as they already had their D'Angelicos and were happy with them; however, they encouraged D'Aquisto and spread the word about the fine guitars he was creating.

By 1967 the orders for guitars reached a satisfactory level. D'Aquisto worked steadily for six years, during which time the family expanded to include Michelle and James II, the fifth and sixth children of the D'Aquisto household. During this time in

James D'Aquisto tapping and testing an instrument in progress.
(Photo courtesy of T. Olsen.)

A D'Aquisto New Yorker, circa 1966. *(Photo courtesy of James D'Aquisto and the author's archive.)*

Huntington, he also took on a new partner for a new string business.

D'Aquisto relocated to Farmingdale, also on Long Island, in 1973 to manufacture his own strings and to continue his lutherie. He was there for four years before moving to Greenport, New York. Although Greenport offered the peaceful atmosphere D'Aquisto desired, the town was initially reluctant to allow him to build a little shop behind his new home, so he was forced to drive to his Farmingdale shop to work on the instruments. Soon the town of Greenport assented to D'Aquisto's request for a shop, however, and it was at that shop in Greenport that D'Aquisto practiced his artistry until his death.

Amid all of the business and artistic pressures D'Aquisto experienced in his earlier years, another more serious and long-lasting problem appeared: he began experiencing symptoms of epilepsy.

A D'Aquisto New Yorker in for adjustment in the late 1970s. *(Photo courtesy of T. Olsen.)*

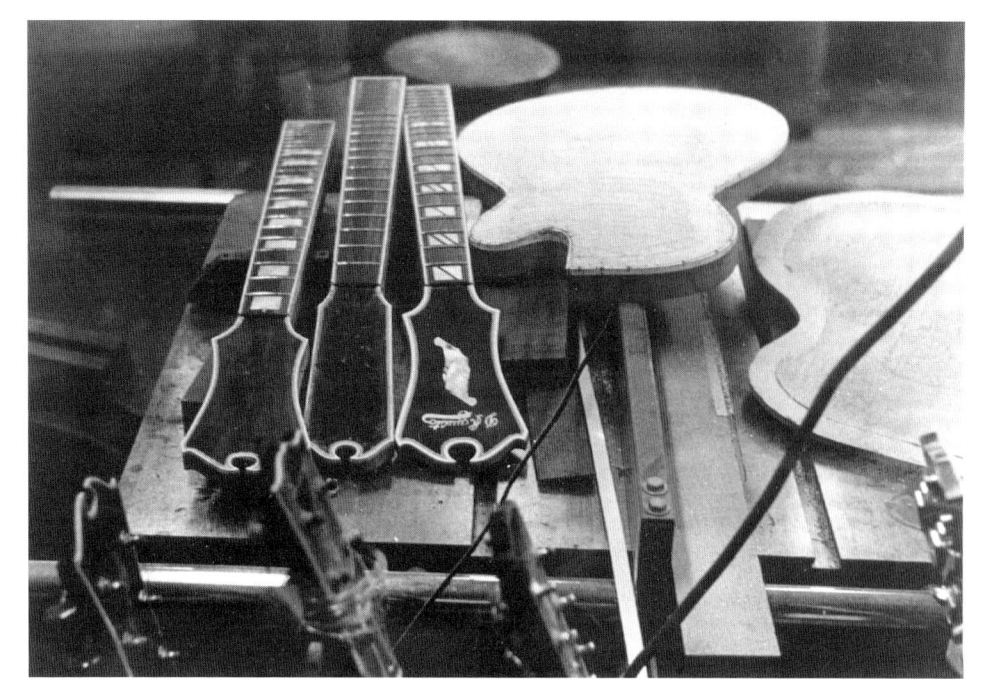

Necks and bodies of various D'Aquisto instruments being readied for completion in the late 1970s. *(Photo courtesy of T. Olsen.)*

Mary D'Aquisto remembered:

> His sickness had always been a terrible cloud. As he got older it seemed to take him a few days longer to "come back." We didn't recognize it until he was in his late twenties, a little after John died. He had a very bad concussion when he was nine, another one in a car accident when he was about 20, and another accident on the Long Island Railroad. It always bothered me a lot—made me sad and worrisome.

Despite the complexities of epilepsy, D'Aquisto could be astonishingly optimistic about his affliction:

> I actually think it has helped me a great deal. After a seizure I need to recover and I have a lot of time to think, which can be

> good or bad. At times I think of the things that are unjust, such as living under a standard where many do not recognize ability, and many with no ability wind up rich! I always thought it was the people that couldn't do anything that invented money. But I also get excited to get back to work, and I come back with even more drive and enthusiasm, and usually some new ideas to try on the guitars. They are something I can leave behind and a way that I can help make the world a bit better.

Despite the epilepsy, which D'Aquisto endured for the balance of his life, the last ten years of his life saw some of his most brilliant contributions to arch-top guitar construction. Having been "successor to D'Angelico" certainly had its advantages; very possibly there would never have been such a thing as a D'Aquisto guitar had it not been for D'Aquisto's apprenticeship with D'Angelico. But throughout D'Aquisto's career as a luthier, he was forced to navigate the waters between the instruments players ordered and the instruments he longed to create—perhaps a situation endemic to all artists and artisans whose first works experience favor.

During the decade of the 1980s, D'Aquisto longed to simplify his instruments but met with reticence from players who wanted instruments that looked like what they pictured in their mind's eye an arch-top f-hole cutaway guitar should look like. D'Aquisto felt trapped:

> I made changes as I discovered them in all of the musical aspects of the guitars—carving and all of that—but I was tired of all of the binding and pearl, and I'd discovered that taking wood away to put in pearl and plastic didn't make any sense musically. But the guys wanted a certain look, so if I wanted to fill orders I couldn't experiment too much, and I didn't like that.

Slowly D'Aquisto began the process of change, incarnating his vision in new designs especially in this last decade of his life. It was also during this period that his instruments gained their greatest notoriety. D'Aquisto's reputation as the world's preeminent arch-top builder became popularized as the cost of, and enthusiasm for, his unique instruments skyrocketed, and a phalanx of younger builders looked to him for insight and inspiration.

Despite the acclaim, respect, and financial benefits of his well-deserved success, the manifestations of epilepsy paid no heed and worsened as D'Aquisto aged. For most of his life D'Aquisto dealt with the travails of epilepsy and was constantly plagued both with the affliction and with the side effects from the prescription drugs he took to lessen the effects of the seizures. As the years passed, D'Aquisto became somewhat haunted by a premonition that he, like D'Angelico, would not live to see his 60th birthday. D'Aquisto's intuition about his life was as astute as it was about his instruments. While in Corona, California, supervising the production of a line of Fender guitars that were to bear his name,

Fine arch-top luthier Steven Andersen studies a D'Aquisto Excel from 1970 (built for jazz legend Joe Pass) at the Guild of American Luthiers conference in 1995. (*Photo courtesy of Joseph Johnson.*)

D'Aquisto complained of feeling poorly and returned to his hotel room to rest. He never awoke.

James L. D'Aquisto was pronounced dead on Tuesday, April 18, 1995, from an apparent epileptic seizure experienced during the previous night. He was buried in the Holy Sepulcher Cemetery, Coram, Long Island, the following Monday. He was survived by his loving wife Phyllis; five daughters, Paula Ardito, Lisa D'Aquisto, Pamela Giordano, Jamie Lynn Giordano, and Michelle Burke; a son, James L. D'Aquisto II; his mother Mary; his brother Joseph; and eight grandchildren.

†

In Loving Memory of

JAMES L. D'AQUISTO
April 18, 1995

The Lord is my Shepherd; I shall not want. In verdant pastures He gives me repose; Before restful waters He leads me; He refreshes my soul. He guides me in right paths for His name's sake. Even though I walk in the dark valley I fear no evil; for you are at my side, with your rod and your staff that give me courage. You spread a table for me in the sight of my foes; you anoint my head with oil; my cup overflows. Only goodness and kindness follow me all the days of my life; And I shall dwell in the house of the Lord for years to come.

F. DANIEL MOLONEY'S
LAKE FUNERAL HOME
132 Ronkonkoma Avenue
Lake Ronkonkoma, NY
(516) 588-1515

From D'Aquisto's funeral.
(Courtesy of the author's archive.)

4

The Instruments

By refining and expanding and making changes to enhance the performance of his instruments, D'Aquisto was beacon-like in his vision as he cleared the arch-top guitar of the dust of tradition. He modernized and evolved his works with standards aimed at producing responsive musical tools. Yet, the term "modernized" somehow implies suitability for present-day standards, and in that sense his works transcended such a level of thought and purpose. Just as D'Angelico began copying Gibson and then went onward, D'Aquisto at first copied D'Angelico and then continued down the path of refinement. Had he merely aped D'Angelico, he would not have been the severe artist to which his instruments bear testament. D'Aquisto realized this:

> When I worked for John a lot of the guys would tease me by saying, "Does this kid really know what he's doing?"—meaning me. John eventually got angry at that and said, "He's going to be better than me!" The first time I heard that I flipped. I thought, "Now that I have his confidence he can have me for life!" I never had the slightest notion of ever building my own guitars. John taught me to help him, and that was what I was there to do. If John hadn't been torn from me I'd still be with him; and though it had to happen in a terrible way, I see now that had he not been ripped from my life I'd have never been myself or created an instrument.
>
> After the first 15 guitars I got tired of people calling my guitar a D'Angelico. It bothered me because they were my guitars,

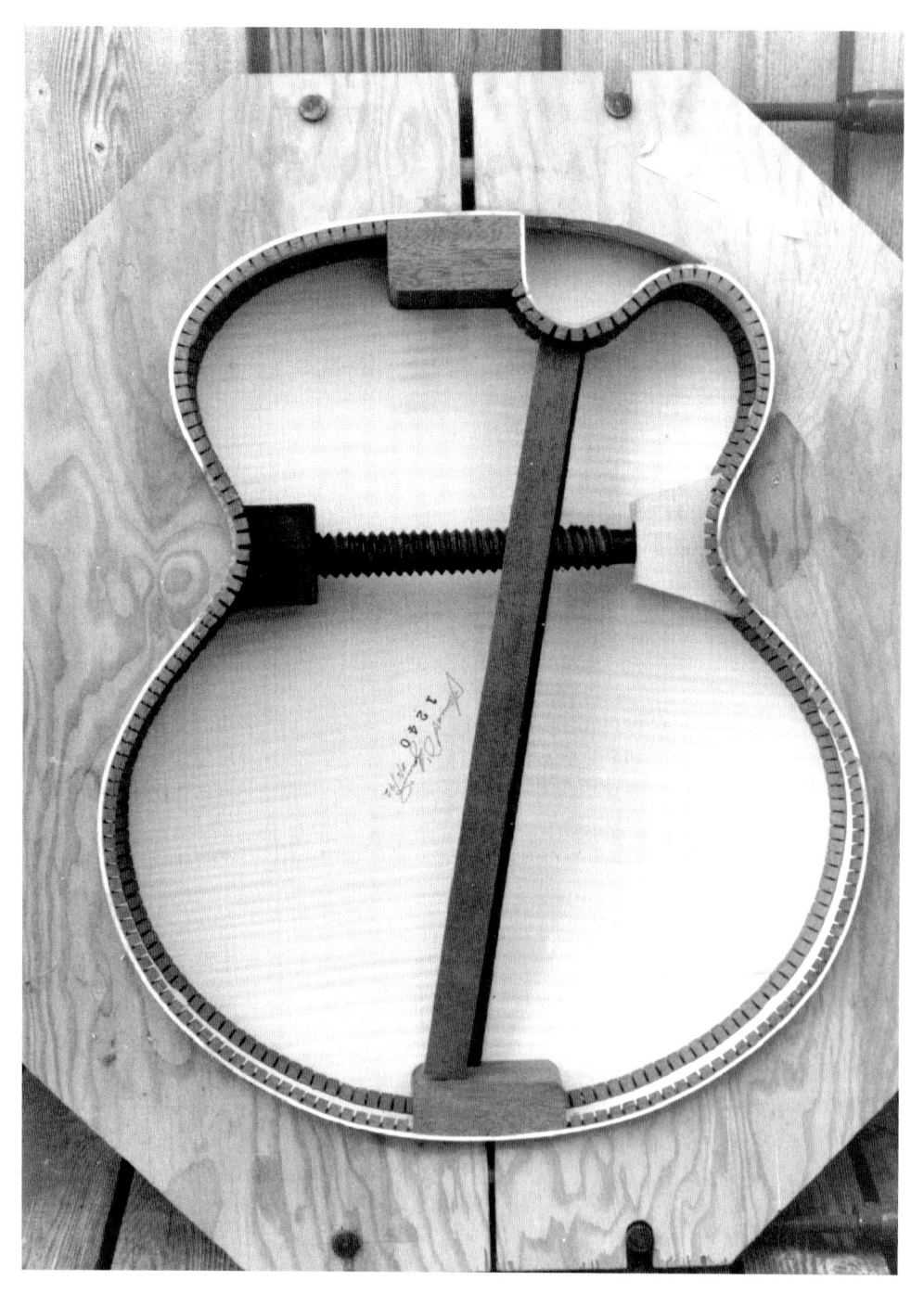

The completed and signed back of D'Aquisto guitar #1240, still in the form. *(Photo by Tim Olsen; previously published in* American Luthier *magazine; reprinted by permission.)*

Forms in D'Aquisto's shop. *(Photo courtesy of T. Olsen.)*

and it wasn't fair to John. I wanted to give myself some sense of identity, but I also didn't want to stray too far from John's design because it was so good.

In a sense, D'Aquisto did exactly what D'Angelico did: he took what he considered to be the best of the period and then experimented to improve the instruments with new ideas and a personality. D'Aquisto was perhaps the first to attempt to build a specific tone into an instrument, as he came to understand that the archtop design offered a plethora of options for altering details, which could impact an instrument's tone. Players who ordered instruments from D'Aquisto would bring them back and ask if there was a way of altering the instrument to produce a slightly different tone color, and D'Aquisto would tackle the notion. This sort of dialogue with musicians was an important part of D'Aquisto's process; so as he began experimenting with bridges, tailpieces, carving, bracing, neck angles, and so forth, he made discoveries that enhanced the capabilities of his instruments.

A completed solid-bodied instrument from the late 1970s. (Photo courtesy of T. Olsen.)

CONSTRUCTION

Although D'Aquisto made not only arch-top guitars but also flat-top instruments, plywood-bodied instruments, solid and hollow-solid instruments, and mandolins, he is most revered for his carved-top acoustic guitars—the style of guitar D'Aquisto felt was the ultimate instrument. Though not intended to be a detailed technical "play-by-play" description that would enable someone to replicate the process followed by D'Aquisto in creating one of his instruments, the following discusses a number of the procedures involved in creating a D'Aquisto carved guitar.

A 1985 D'Aquisto New Yorker Classic. Note the maple binding. *(Photo courtesy of Glen Delman and the author's archive.)*

(Many aspects of the following procedure can be viewed in Frederick Cohen's award-winning film about D'Aquisto, *The New Yorker Special*.) For a more detailed description, refer to to one of the fine articles by Tim Olsen in *American Lutherie* listed in the bibliography.

D'Aquisto began by selecting the sides, which were almost always made from European maple, as was the back. The top was selected from either European or Engelmann spruce. It was this combination of woods that typified almost all of D'Aquisto's carved instruments, for it was this combination of woods which best suited his understanding of a superior arch-top guitar.

D'Aquisto's choice of a particular piece of wood (or actually, *pieces* of wood, as both the tops and the backs are each fashioned from two pieces of matching woods) for the back was made irrespective of the sides with which it would mate, but its tonal prop-

Bending the sides for a flat-top instrument. *(Photo courtesy of the author's archive.)*

The form in which D'Aquisto receives the matched backs. *(Photo courtesy of the author's archive.)*

erties determined whether it would be used for a 17-inch or 18-inch guitar (the backs that made for a brighter tone color were utilized for the larger instruments). Once the back was selected, a top would be chosen to work with the already chosen back, and it was the density of the top that was the foremost criterion utilized for its selection.

D'Aquisto then selected the piece of wood that would become the neck of the instrument. This wood, frequently sugar maple, was selected for its visually aesthetic relationship with the figure of the wood chosen for the back of the instrument.

Most of D'Aquisto's instruments measured either 17 inches or 18 inches at the lower bout, and he had created molds (made in two halves) within which he fashioned his instruments. The 18-inch mold was both wider and longer than the 17-inch mold, and both were designed by D'Aquisto to have a small gap between the halves (of approximately one inch). This feature enabled D'Aquisto to alter the width of the upper bout while keeping the lower bout a constant, which translated musically as having the flexibility to make the instrument's voice smoother with a wider upper bout.

The sides of the instrument were wet and then bent over a hot pipe to match the shape of the chosen mold. D'Aquisto did all of his bending by feel as some pieces of wood lent themselves to different depths of a cutaway (almost all of D'Aquisto's instruments were cutaways). Mahogany endblocks were then glued to the sides, as were side reinforcements (made of spruce) and mahogany linings. The sides were then put into the mold.

After this, the two pieces of wood that would become the back were joined, as were the two pieces of wood that would become the top (D'Aquisto used Titebond glue for all of the gluing of his instruments). These were then rough-carved on a router, each model (17-inch or 18-inch) having its own distinctive template, and left rather thick (approximately ¾-inch in the middle) so as to allow for greater flexibility during the hand carving process. These pieces were next cut to an oversize guitar outline and laid

The first roughing out of a D'Aquisto top. *(Photo by Tim Olsen; previously published in* American Luthier *magazine; reprinted by permission.)*

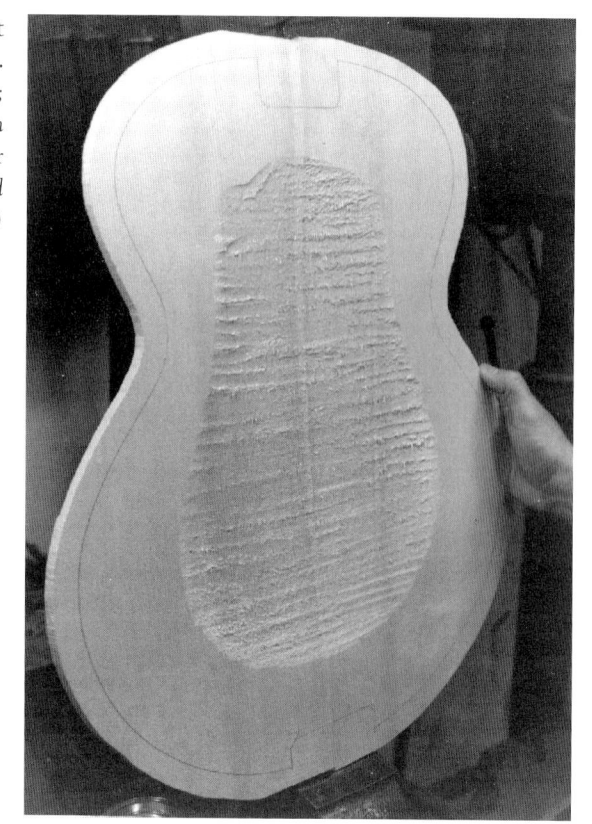

The machine D'Aquisto used to rough carve the backs. The second and third (from the left) forms duplicate what the operator does in the first form. *(Photo courtesy of the author's archive.)*

right-side-up in the router, whereupon the outside arch was routed and the newly created raised ridge was trimmed off with a table saw. The same piece was then flipped over and an inside arch was routed.

Once the plates for the top and back were so fashioned, they were aligned to the centerline of the form and pinned to the blocks with brads (binding would cover the holes once the brads were removed). The blocks, lining, and sides were traced into each plate to indicate the gluing surface—an area which was to be left flat during the carving process. It was at this point that D'Aquisto determined the shape and height of the arch of the top of the instrument—an important feature that greatly impacted the sound of the instrument. The position of the bridge was calculated and marked with pencil on the center seam, followed by the tracings of the sound holes, which were determined by this center seam.

D'Aquisto tested his tops and backs by feel. *(Photo by Tim Olsen; previously published in* American Luthier *magazine; reprinted by permission.)*

D'Aquisto's carving planes. *(Photo by Tim Olsen; previously published in* American Luthier *magazine; reprinted by permission.)*

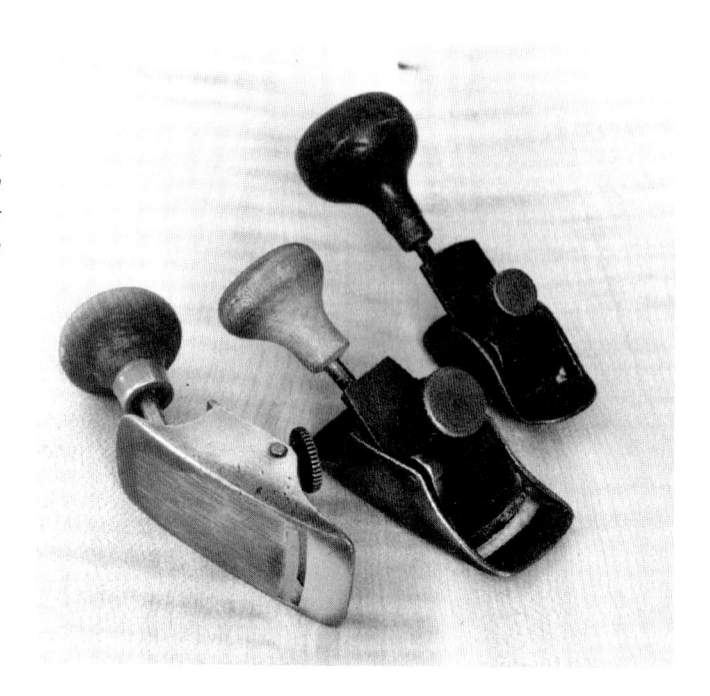

Next, the inside shaping of the top was carved until the top was of a consistent thickness, at which point the sound holes were cut out, using a jigsaw. The inside shaping of the arch of the back was then formed with the same round-bottom plane utilized in shaping the top and further refined with oval scrapers. Interestingly enough, D'Aquisto did not take measurements, but laid a straightedge at various angles across the plate to check for the desired symmetries. The plate was then sanded, given a serial number, and signed by D'Aquisto.

After the side assembly (including blocks and linings) had been trued with a long plane, the back was glued in place and clamped. Then the ever-important task of shaping the inside arch of the top was undertaken, also utilizing planes and scrapers and the straightedge. It was at this point that D'Aquisto began tapping and planing the top.

D'Aquisto next began work on the bracing structure, another meaningful aspect to the prospective sound of the instrument.

He used Sitka spruce (favoring its stiffness) for the braces—two pieces that had been adjacent in the board from which they were taken—and then made determinations regarding their width (the greater the width of the brace, the brighter the sound of the instrument). Next, the angle of the braces was determined in relationship to the sound of the top and the brace itself and to

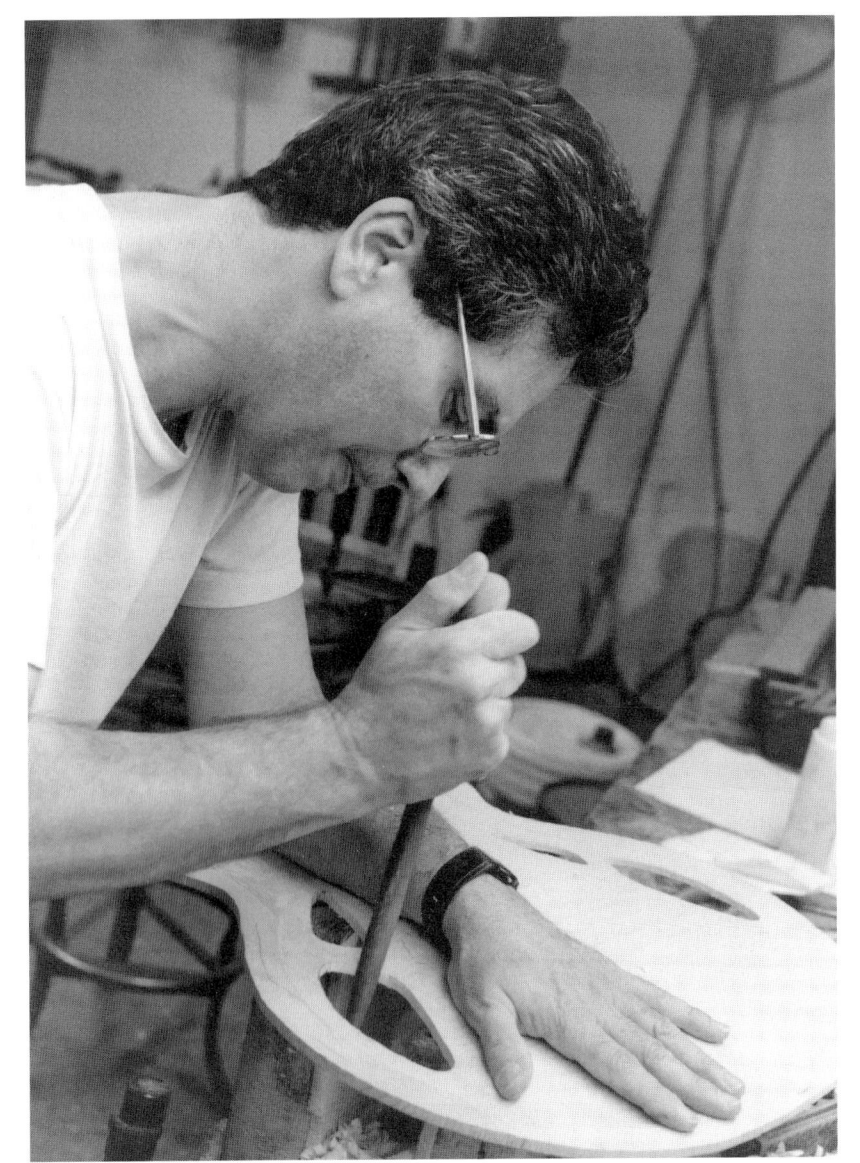

Rasping the sound holes. *(Photo by Tim Olsen; previously published in* American Luthier *magazine; reprinted by permission.)*

D'Aquisto makes use of the light as he completes a top. *(Photo by Tim Olsen; previously published in* American Luthier *magazine; reprinted by permission.)*

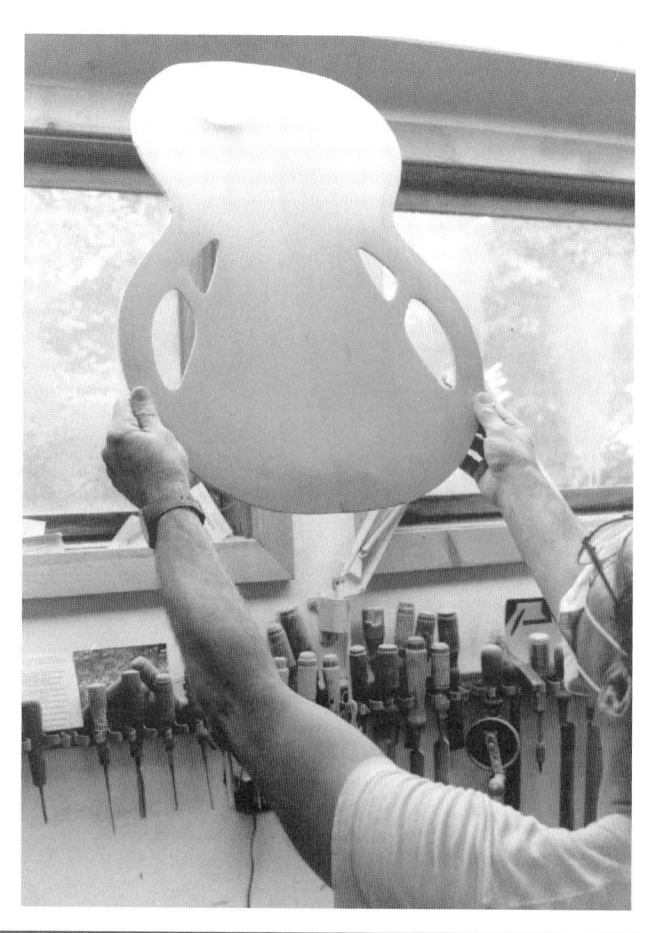

D'Aquisto studies the shadow of a back to determine the next procedure. *(Photo by Tim Olsen; previously published in* American Luthier *magazine; reprinted by permission.)*

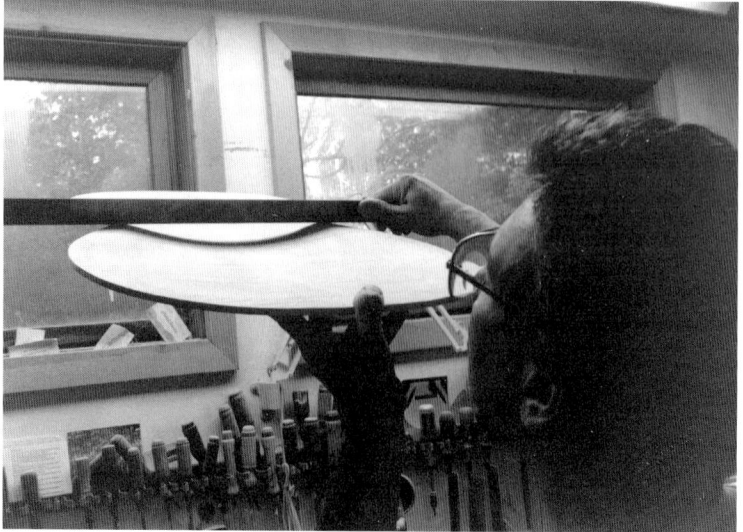

the position of the sound holes; that angle was then marked at the four corner positions of the braces. The shape of the top was transferred (marked by pencil) to the side of each brace, and the braces were sawn and rasped accordingly and then fitted more specifically with the aid of a scraper. D'Aquisto felt that this procedure of fitting the braces played a significant role in the prospective performance of a completed instrument.

The braces were glued to each other and to the top of the instrument at the same time. Next, the top was glued to the back and side assembly, and the remaining wood from the original oversize guitar outline was removed with the bandsaw and rasp.

The neck was the next component of the instrument to receive attention, as a groove was cut into the neck blank to receive a truss rod made of $3/16$-inch steel. The rod was inserted

D'Aquisto files a brace. *(Photo by Tim Olsen; previously published in* American Luthier *magazine; reprinted by permission.)*

D'Aquisto ponders a bracing pattern in his shop in Greenport, New York.
(Photo by Tim Olsen; previously published in American Luthier *magazine; reprinted by permission.)*

THE INSTRUMENTS 117

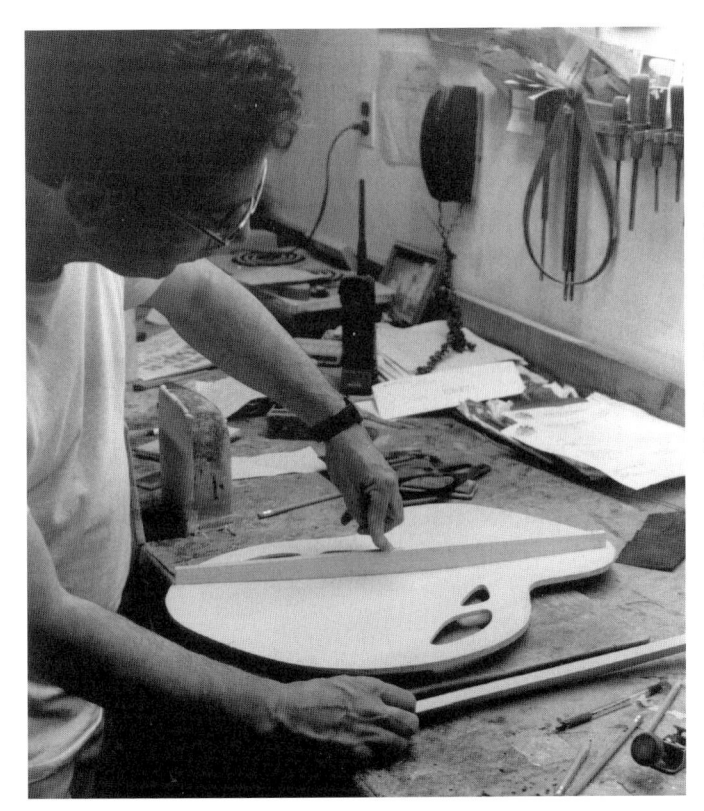

D'Aquisto fitting a brace to a future Solo model instrument. *(Photo by Tim Olsen; previously published in* American Luthier *magazine; reprinted by permission.)*

D'Aquisto clamps a brace. *(Photo by Tim Olsen; previously published in* American Luthier *magazine; reprinted by permission.)*

into the neck and made adjustable from the peghead end. Then a maple extension, used as a support for the fingerboard where it came over the body, was dovetailed onto the neck blank. The peghead wings along with the fretboard extension were glued at the same time.

The fretboard on D'Aquisto instruments was fashioned from ebony and was prepared by cutting it to the finished shape of the neck (save the width of the binding strips, if the instrument had fingerboard binding, which was added to cover the ends of the frets). It was at this time that the peghead veneer and fretboard were glued onto the neck/headpiece assembly. The headpiece was then shaped to its final silhouette with the use of saws and files, and the shape and contour of the fretboard were finalized with the use of a plane and sanding blocks, followed by the creation of the fret slots and subsequent fretting of the instrument.

D'Aquisto used both plastic and wooden bindings around his necks and bodies, each of which had their own specific procedures for application. D'Aquisto readied the tops and backs for the reception of the binding (although in his last years, D'Aquisto did create some instruments that featured no binding). The top and back were brought down to a uniform ¼-inch around the perimeter of the body, and the body depth (typically 3 inches) was concretized. The binding ledge was then routed by passing the body around a "binding-ledge-specific" piece of machinery, which left all of the linings untouched. The plastic bindings were applied with clear nitrate dissolved in acetone, and held in place by a tied cotton cord (at which point the instrument looked not unlike a mummy!). The wooden bindings were affixed with Titebond glue.

After some final touches to the top of the instrument (featuring the employment of planes, scrapers, and sanding), the next major task was that of setting the neck, a complex procedure which involved taking into account the arch of the top and the desired amount of pressure to achieve the musical function D'Aquisto desired from a particular instrument. The dovetailing of the neck onto the body required great precision, not only in the cutting of the body mortice, but even more so in the fitting of the neck to the body. D'Aquisto noted that this was always a significant moment in the birth of an instrument, as an error at this point could literally ruin all of the work that had preceded it.

With the neck in place, next came the final carving of the back, similar in procedure to the finishing process of the top. D'Aquisto employed his tapping technique to note how the relationship between the top and back was developing, and he made

D'Aquisto putting binding on a solid body. *(Photo courtesy of Joshua McClure/ Island Color Photo.)*

adjustments germane to his goals. Though the top of the instrument produced its fundamental sound, it was the back of the instrument that shaped that sound: a heavier-backed instrument favored the higher range, whereas a lighter-backed one was more friendly to the lower range.

Final touches to the neck followed (more rasping, scraping, and sanding), as did the fine sanding which readied the instrument for finishing. His procedure for finishing was similar to D'Angelico's: three coats of nitrocellulose lacquer, light sanding, and shading or sunbursting (if any), followed by ten or so coats of additional lacquer (with light sanding between every three coats). The instrument would then dry for several weeks before finally being wet-sanded and buffed with a buffing compound.

The final pieces such as the tailpiece, bridge, and pickguard were fashioned from ebony (both Macassar and Gabon ebony were utilized). The tailpiece was fashioned from a single piece of ebony with a chiseled string ramp and holes drilled, through

D'Aquisto pickguard as the binding dries. (*Photo courtesy of the author's archive.*)

which the strings would pass. The bridge was also a significant contributor to the prospective tone of the instrument. D'Aquisto had done much experimentation with bridges—various sizes, widths, lengths, densities, and configurations—and he came to favor relatively wide (1-inch to 1¼-inch widths) and heavy bridges. Also, D'Aquisto liked to begin with large bridges and let the customer break an instrument in before doing any further custom tailoring of the sound. D'Aquisto instruments took time to develop and consistently ripened as they aged.

COMPARISON WITH D'ANGELICO INSTRUMENTS

The differences between D'Angelicos and D'Aquistos were subtle but numerous. As detailed above, D'Aquisto utilized mahogany linings in place of D'Angelico's favored basswood. D'Angelico often used domestic maple for the backs and sides and Sitka spruce for the tops, whereas D'Aquisto used only European maple for the back and sides and only European or Engelmann spruce for the tops.

Bridge designs were one of D'Aquisto's first major experiments. As he changed their sizes and masses, and deleted the pearl inlays that were so common on D'Angelico's instruments, he noticed that these new designs produced subtle tonal differences in the instruments. On his last instruments, D'Aquisto was utilizing a three-piece bridge configuration, which incorporated a tone bar that created an interface between the top and bottom portions of the bridge.

D'Aquisto began altering the f-holes and headpieces of his instruments in 1967. The f-holes became s-holes, reminiscent of D'Angelico's straight f-holes, which appeared on his Excel model guitar in the mid-1930s, and not unlike the Stradivari templates. Also, the headpiece became a smoother version of the broken-scroll pediment design.

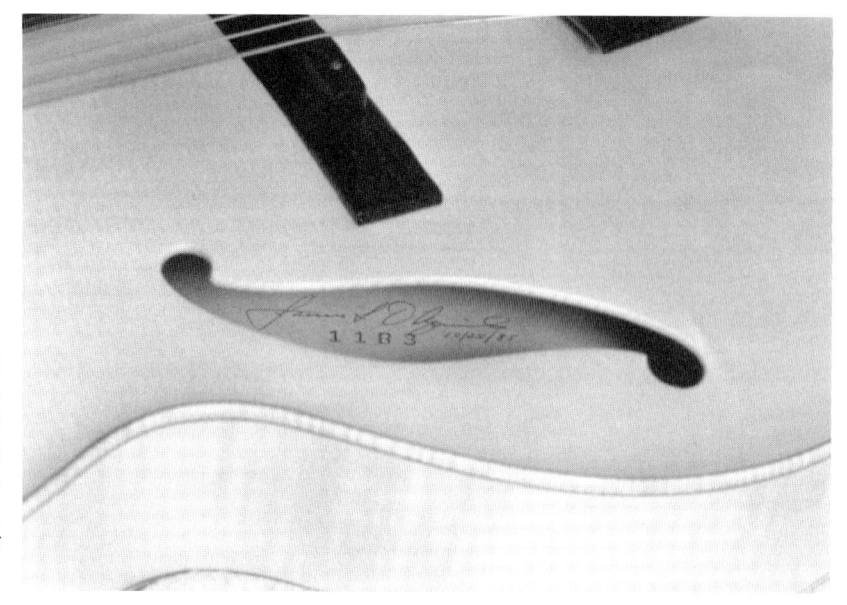

The signature, date, and serial number on the inside of the first D'Aquisto New Yorker Classic. *(Photo courtesy of Glen Delman.)*

D'Aquisto also experimented with the tailpiece (fashioned from brass, as were D'Angelico's) and began affixing shorter versions of his metal tailpiece to his instruments. Most of these variations occurred between 1967 and 1969. It was during the early 1970s that D'Aquisto began fashioning his tailpieces from ebony (for musical reasons). On instruments from the late 1980s onward, he made the string guide portion in the shape of a **V** to provide for longer D- and G-strings.

D'Aquisto made the switch from plastic pickguards to ebony pickguards at the same time he went to ebony tailpieces. His fingerboard widths became steadily wider (though of course any width was obtainable, depending on the hand size and playing style of the prospective customer) and also somewhat flatter. D'Aquisto's ideas regarding cosmetic features went in the opposite direction of D'Angelico's. As his instruments evolved, D'Aquisto gradually began making use of fewer layers of body binding, and he encouraged his customers to leave the fingerboard blank of ornamentation. D'Aquisto went for cleanliness and simplicity of design, as his last models exemplify.

MODELS

At the beginning of D'Aquisto's career one would have been hard-pressed to tell the difference between a D'Angelico and a D'Aquisto guitar, but by the end of his life one would have been equally puzzled trying to find any similarities, especially visually.

In his early years, D'Aquisto's model designations, like his guitars, were the same as D'Angelico's—the Excel and the New Yorker (the main distinction between the two being the style of inlay and the quantity of binding). Yet, just as with D'Angelico, these models were more of the family of guidelines than they were specific concrete descriptions. D'Aquisto's instruments

Instruments in for repair and adjustment at the D'Aquisto shop. Note the D'Aquisto classical and flap-top oval hole. *(Photo courtesy of the author's archive.)*

were perhaps even more highly customized than D'Angelico's, especially in the realm of their prospective musical intent. Thus, the model designations are not terribly helpful in elucidating a particular alteration or design variation—cosmetics perhaps being the only exception.

Throughout his career, D'Aquisto created carved-top instruments in 16-inch, 17-inch, and 18-inch sizes (with the same subtle size variations as the D'Angelico instruments) and a very few even smaller ones; instruments with different types of sound holes—D'Angelico-styled f-holes, s-holes, and both elliptical and oval sound holes; cutaway and noncutaway instruments; and 6-stringed and 12-stringed instruments. In the springtime of 1985, D'Aquisto completed a 16-inch oval-hole 12-stringed instrument, which he finished with all wooden bindings (in place of the previously used celluloid); he referred to it as the "Classic." Later the following year he made an 18-inch New Yorker with the same

D'Aquisto playing a small oval-hole instrument he created for folk/pop singer Melanie in 1972 (#1601). *(Photo courtesy of the author's archive.)*

cosmetic features, including a maple headpiece veneer, free of ornamentation save the D'Aquisto name scripted in pearl at the apex of the headpiece. This "New Yorker Classic" was a radical departure aesthetically, a departure D'Aquisto both welcomed and nourished (many of his customers cheering right along).

The ledger books note that in 1989 D'Aquisto premiered another new model he named the "Avant Garde" (first referred to as the "Deco"), which featured the same simplicity and binding configuration as the New Yorker Classic, but with additional unique features: elliptical sound holes (which D'Aquisto had used as far back as the 1970s), open spaces carved into the headpiece, a Chrysler Building–like truss rod cover, and more. Next came the "Solo" model in 1992 (first referred to as the "Savant"), which featured four sound holes and a variation on the carved-out headpiece design. After that came the "Centura" and "Centura Deluxe" in 1993 and finally the "Advance," which was highly futuristic in its visual presentation, to the point of featuring sound hole covers.

All throughout his career D'Aquisto made refinements and embellishments to his instruments to enhance their musical capabilities, and it would be as unfair as it would be inaccurate to imply that each of these new models represented a "leap" in quality. Indeed the later models were exemplary musical tools, and many feel they were among his finest creations, but their visual differences from the earlier instruments were more dramatic than were their musical differences—although that is not to imply that their voices didn't differ from those of their ancestors.

As was previously mentioned, D'Aquisto created instruments other than the carved-top guitars. D'Aquisto began creating flat-top instruments in 1973, fashioned from the same materials as were the carved-top instruments. They were available in styles similar to the Martin Guitar Company's model designations "Dreadnought" and "Grand Auditorium," but the ledger books indicate that D'Aquisto only created them from 1973 through 1983. D'Aquisto also created a very few classical-style nylon-stringed guitars, as well as three mandolins.

D'Aquisto tests a recently completed solid body in 1992. *(Photo by Tim Olsen; previously published in* American Luthier *magazine; reprinted by permission.)*

D'Aquisto with the body for a classical instrument. *(Photo by Joshua McClure/Island Color Photo.)*

D'Aquisto also created strictly electric instruments, such as plywood hollow-body electrics similar in design to the Gibson Company's ES-175 model guitar. His first plywood guitars featured bodies created by United Guitars (the same supplier D'Angelico had used). D'Aquisto fashioned the necks from solid maple and completed them with the pickups and electronic configurations the customer ordered. From 1967 until 1979 he obtained the bodies for the plywood instruments (made from nine-ply laminated birch) from Hagstrom, a company with which he became associated as designer for an instrument that never came to fruition. From 1979 onward, D'Aquisto created templates for a top and back, which were pressed by the same company that pressed the plywood tops and backs for the Gibson Company's instruments. These instruments (post-1979) incorporated solid maple sides hand-bent by D'Aquisto, as well as maple necks made in the same manner as D'Aquisto's acoustic instruments.

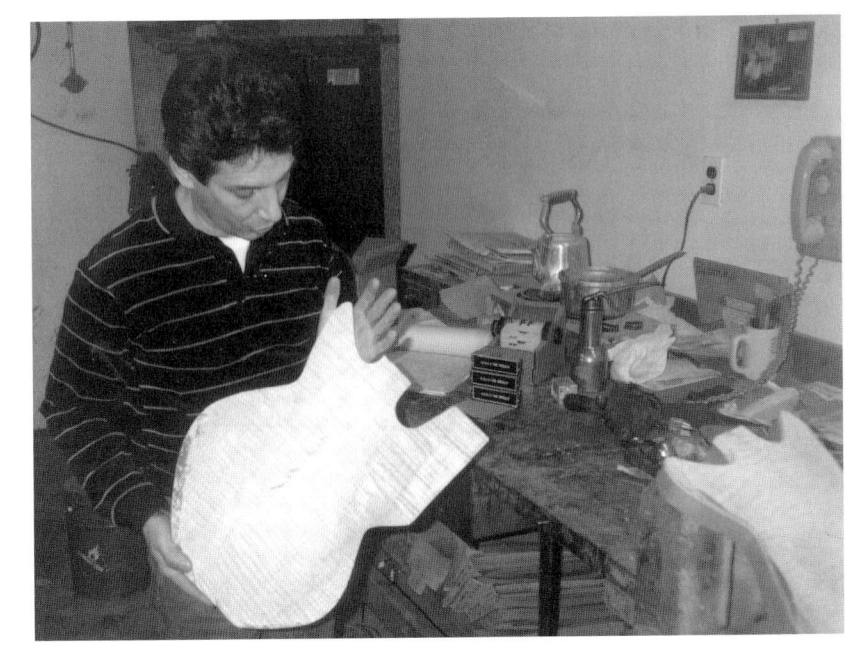

A body in the rough for a guitar controller for a synthesizer, late 1980s. (*Photo courtesy of the author's archive.*)

D'Aquisto's other electric instruments included solid maple single-cutaway models similar to the Gibson Company's Les Paul model (some with spruce tops), the last of which were styled after D'Aquisto's acoustic Centura model; and hollow/solid-bodied, single- and double-cutaway instruments fashioned from mahogany and maple, as well as other variations on these themes.

ARTISTIC PERSPECTIVES

Though D'Aquisto created all styles of instruments, he was primarily referred to as a "jazz guitar" maker. The "jazz guitar" moniker, as discussed earlier, is a reference to the style of guitar that became popularized by the style of music with which it was associated. Given that D'Aquisto also created rock guitars (solid and hollow/solid instruments), folk guitars (flat-tops), and classical guitars (nylon-stringed flat-tops), the title he elected to place on his letterhead was most apt: "Custom Guitar Maker." As D'Aquisto explained, "People don't understand that I can make any kind of guitar. The reason I don't make a lot of solid bodies is because I don't get a lot of orders for them."

Many who did order instruments from D'Aquisto needed to be educated about them in order to fully realize the qualities and capabilities of these responsive musical tools. D'Aquisto was striving for a perfect match between guitar and owner:

D'Aquisto's business card. (*Courtesy of James D'Aquisto and the author's archive.*)

516-477-2017

JAMES L. D'AQUISTO

GUITAR MAKER

P.O. BOX 259
GREENPORT, N.Y. 11944

> When I make a guitar I have to talk to the player to find out what they are like so I know what that guitar should sound like. When I hear a player talk, I know what they'll be listening for and how they'll use the instrument. I make guitars for individuals, so each instrument is an individual for an individual.

It sounds simple, and in truth it is. Individuality is inherent in each human being, but its recognition and assertion are only brought to fruition with constant attention and effort—precious things in art, which D'Aquisto nurtured authentically. There is no blueprint or prescription for producing quality art—it is a process, not a craft, as D'Aquisto knew:

> Making guitars is not an exact science; it goes way beyond that. I'm not into measurements. Most of the questions I get regarding how many millimeters the top on an 18-inch guitar is, are not grounded on any musical thing. It all depends on the piece of wood, the use of the guitar, and what sound I am trying to build into the guitar. As far as breaking it down into a theory like people have done with Stradivari, they had to do that to explain it to themselves. All he did was carve it, feel it, and relate to it in a way that those researchers could never understand.
>
> I'm not an expert on detailed scientific structures of wood—I never even consider that. Art is not confined to rules. The people with theories can rarely build anything. There are no definite rules to my method of creating an instrument. I build upon the ideas I learned in the beginning with John and, since his death, the discoveries I make with my own instruments.

D'Aquisto did what he did because he knew what to do. It sounds a bit elliptical, yet it was true. His advice to other artists, notwithstanding the medium, was simple as well:

> I always tried to put all I believed in into my work. It can only work if one strives to better oneself. I never tried to be better than John. He was D'Angelico trying to make a D'Angelico guitar. I am D'Aquisto making my guitar. It is not on the same level as a competitive sport or something. The only competi-

tion that should take place is with yourself. I want to share that I make good instruments for players who appreciate and respect them. By realizing the instrument, they realize me. This is a way I can hopefully make the world a better place.

More than a few find the world a better place for the lives of John D'Angelico and James L. D'Aquisto—for who they were and for all of the beautiful instruments they created. D'Angelico and D'Aquisto were not unlike the Amati and Stradivari of guitar makers: brilliant artists that have truly graced the earth with the most eloquent of instruments. D'Angelico and D'Aquisto were perhaps the preeminent arch-top guitar makers of the twentieth century, and their artistry will benefit humanity for centuries to come.

A photo session of a completed instrument at the studio of long-time D'Aquisto photographer Josh McClure. *(Photo courtesy of the author's archive.)*

D'Aquisto's shop in Greenport: Brilliant art from a modified garage. *(Photo courtesy of the author's archive.)*

OTHER VENTURES

Aside from creating instruments, D'Aquisto had been involved in several other music-related projects. The first strings made with the D'Aquisto label were made by two fellows who had originally formed the Archaic String Company and who had made the first D'Angelico strings for John D'Angelico. John D'Addario Sr. bought into the Archaic Company, which became the Darco Company. D'Aquisto recalls:

> D'Addario bought into Archaic, but whenever I wanted something done I spoke with Albert and Gino [the originators of Archaic]. They started Archaic in a 15-foot-by-15-foot shop that had four string machines. Albert's family had been stringmakers for generations in Italy and they did fine work.

When the D'Addarios left Darco, the newly formed D'Addario Company asked D'Aquisto if they could make his strings. D'Aquisto assented and the strings were distributed by

Early D'Aquisto string packaging. (*Courtesy of James D'Aquisto and the author's archive.*)

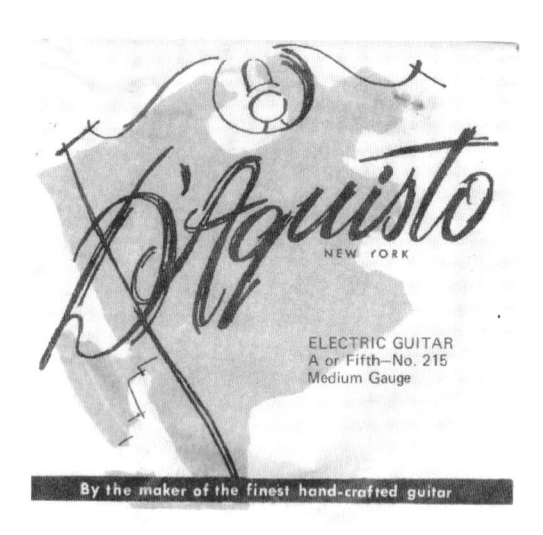

D'Aquisto's own distributing company, DAQ Musical Distributing, Inc. Later on, after various shifts in the D'Addario business, D'Aquisto signed a five-year contract with D'Addario to make and distribute strings bearing the D'Aquisto name. At the close of that contract in 1984, D'Aquisto went out of the string business until 1989, when he introduced a complete line of strings called D'Aquisto Micro-Flex Strings (still available as of 1998).

D'Aquisto's first experience in designing an instrument for another company occurred in 1966 when Hagstrom, a Gulf & Western company, requested a design for an arch-top guitar they intended to build in Sweden. D'Aquisto recalled:

> I met with Carl Hagstrom, designed the guitar, and showed them how to make it, right at their shop with the workmen watching me. It never really materialized. The guitar that did emerge was Hagstrom's version of what I had shown them. It was plywood. I had nothing to do with that guitar. They paid me a royalty to put "designed by D'Aquisto" on, and that lasted for about four years.

D'Aquisto designed a guitar line for the Gianinni Guitar Company in São Paulo, Brazil, in the early 1970s. The instru-

An advertisement from D'Aquisto's affiliation with D'Addario. *(Photo courtesy of James D'Aquisto and the author's archive.)*

ments were flat-topped nylon- and steel-stringed guitars, including the unusually shaped nylon-stringed Craviola model. D'Aquisto also designed a guitar, which debuted in 1984, for the Fender Musical Instrument Company. He sent the plans to Fender in California, who shipped them to Japan, where the instruments were being made for a time. The three models manufactured were the Ultra, Elite, and Standard. D'Aquisto was in California meeting with Fender about some new instruments when he died.

D'Aquisto playing a completed New Yorker Classic. Note Hagstrom prototype in the foreground (the second instrument from the left, next to Paul Simon's Excel waiting to be rebound). *(Photo courtesy of the author's archive.)*

D'Aquisto with a prototype for Fender. *(Photo by Joshua McClure/Island Color Photo.)*

CONCLUSION

Memories of the D'As

Al Valenti in 1937 with his New Yorker. *(Photo courtesy of Al Valenti.)*

Memories of the D'As

The following reminiscences are included to shed some different lights on D'Angelico and D'Aquisto—as they were seen by knowledgeable and experienced persons who interacted with them and/or their creations.

Guitarist Alphonse "Al" Valenti was one of the first to premiere D'Angelico instruments throughout the United States, while on tour with the Joe Reichman Orchestra. He has performed and recorded with D'Angelico instruments ever since 1934 and was a close personal friend of John D'Angelico. Mr. Valenti recalled:

> I had a flat-top guitar with an oval sound hole. One day the bridge popped off, so I took the guitar to a local violin maker that also repaired other fretted instruments. Two days after the repair, the bridge popped off again. I took it back, it was repaired, and it came off again!
>
> A friend of mine referred me to another repairman named John D'Angelico, who had a small repair shop at 40 Kenmare Street. I decided to have him do the repair, and when I went back to pick up the guitar he explained to me that the first repairman didn't understand the science of the guitar. I still have this guitar, and after 58 years the bridge repair still holds! D'Angelico's ability was fantastic.
>
> In 1934 I decided to join the musicians' union so I could get better jobs and better pay. A friend of mine said there was an opening for a guitar player in the Joe Reichman band. I got the call to join the band in June of 1934. Being eighteen at the

time, I was thrilled to play professionally. I was soon to meet D'Angelico again. One night two salesmen came by to show me a guitar D'Angelico had just completed. John called it the Excel model, and he wanted my opinion as to how it cut in the rhythm section of the band. I could see it was a beautiful instrument, and when I tried it out the boys in the band noticed that it was a better instrument than the one I'd been using. One of the violin players in the band, who had a music store on the side that handled all of the best makes at the time, said that this guitar ranked supreme above all he'd ever seen.

John made an instrument for me that I began using exclusively. My D'Angelico guitar was with me all the time whenever I played. During September 1937 I received another new guitar from D'Angelico, his New Yorker model with an 18-inch body. I had sent the Excel back to John to have new frets put on. The New Yorker was a beautiful instrument indeed—I still

Al Valenti with his New Yorker, rehearsing in the lobby of a Boston theater with mandolin virtuoso Dave Apollon and actor Ed Wynn, in the autumn of 1940. *(Photo courtesy of Al Valenti.)*

Al Valenti with the D'Angelico New Yorker and Dave Apollon at the Warner Bros. Earle Theater in Washington, D.C. in 1941. *(Photo courtesy of Al Valenti.)*

have this guitar and use it to this day [in 1960 this instrument was transformed into a classical-like instrument by D'Angelico by the thinning of the top and with the addition of a special bridge created to accommodate silkwound and nylon strings]. I was demonstrating the D'Angelico New Yorker and Danelectro amplifiers at the Music Trade Show and Convention in New York in 1949, as I was always so impressed by D'Angelico's works and felt fortunate to promote them.

I remember many times when I had to go to D'Angelico's shop, and I'd see Jimmy D'Aquisto, who was always happy to take care of me whenever I needed help with my guitars. I've always known that Jimmy D'Aquisto could handle any technical problems that confronted any guitar player's instrument, and John D'Angelico felt safe in attesting to that. The proof is all there, that the most logical successor to John D'Angelico was Jimmy D'Aquisto. Between John and Jimmy it was like one big happy family cooperating with one purpose in mind: to attain perfection in whatever they did together.

Johnny Smith is a world-recognized guitarist:

I don't remember who introduced me to John D'Angelico, but I do remember going down to his little shop on Kenmare Street in the Bowery section of New York City. I remember the first time I went down there, as I had seen a number of John's guitars and was naturally very impressed by them; I think this was about 1946. John had his workbench set up in the window and you could see him working away with his chisels as you walked by the shop.

Right away I asked him if he would build me a guitar, with New Yorker ornamentation and a 17-inch body. It was a beautiful blonde instrument, but it was destroyed in a fire. I had gone over to have dinner with [noted jazz guitarist] Mary Osborne and her husband, and when I pulled into the driveway upon my arrival back home, I saw the house was leveled. Everything in it had been destroyed.

A short time later a very dear friend of mine named John Collins loaned me an old D'Angelico from the 1930s which had a very large neck. I fell in love with it, though I had placed another order with D'Angelico to start building me another guitar to replace the one that had been destroyed in the fire. I was so in love with the guitar that John Collins had loaned me that I didn't want to give it back, so I had John D'Angelico build him a guitar and I kept the old D'Angelico from the 1930s. I sold that guitar not too long after my 17-inch New Yorker was completed.

When I first saw that guitar—my second 17-inch New Yorker—I thought it was the most beautiful instrument I had ever seen in my life. It was incredible what this man could do. During the time he was building my guitar I had several occasions when I'd be down there [at the shop], and as he completed a guitar he would always put on a heavy-gauge second-string first and test the instrument by plucking that one string. If John felt it was a really fine instrument, he would leave and return with a bottle of wine, and we'd all toddy to the guitar.

When he finished my guitar I could tell without even hearing it that it was an exceptional instrument—I could sense it and see it. One of the most amazing things I'd seen him do was hand-shape the base of the bridge to contour perfectly the top of the guitar. He put the piece of ebony in a vise and took a file, and he hand-contoured it. He took it out of the vise and just touched it to the top of my guitar, and it was absolutely perfect. I couldn't believe it! I was absolutely amazed—I couldn't imagine anybody could do such a thing.

These instruments [D'Angelicos and D'Aquistos] will become like Stradivarius violins: less available and more valuable, as they should be in the same league with fine concert violins.

I had the greatest respect for Jimmy D'Aquisto, the man that carried on the great traditions of craftsmanship that John bestowed upon him.

The late George Melega had been a broker for D'Angelico and D'Aquisto instruments for more than twenty years, during which time he became acquainted with more than two hundred examples of D'Angelico's and D'Aquisto's works. Mr. Melega was a lifelong fan:

> When I was a little boy studying the guitar I always wanted D'Angelico guitars, and I wanted to meet him, but there was no one to introduce me to him. I started taking lessons in Brooklyn when I was 13, and I always saw the top players using D'Angelicos. I'd always go down to where all the guitar stores were and look in the windows.
>
> In the early 1940s you could get a used Style A or Style B for $90. In those days the New Yorker was $400, the Excel was $275; they were priced like the new Gibson Super 400 and the L-5 [respectively].
>
> I switched to the bass and by the early 1960s I was doing a

lot of record dates. I was single and making a lot of money with all of those record dates, so I started collecting arch-top guitars for fun, like stamps or something. I'd be on the road with Skitch Henderson or Peter Duchin and I'd go into pawn shops and buy them. A lot of the young players had switched over to solid-bodies in the early 1960s and the arch-tops weren't as popular. I started selling them in 1965 just because I thought all these guitars I had accumulated should have homes—so it was then that I just became a broker for them.

I chose D'Angelicos because they were such lovely pieces of art, and it was a challenge to get one. They were just better than anything else—I never heard a bad one, and I heard a lot of them. I've sold about ten a year for the past twenty-two years. They are becoming harder to get now [in the mid-1980s]. When I started with them in the mid-1960s you could find one fairly easily for around $1,200 to $1,500, and they have gone up in price steadily ever since.

Matt Umanov is a dealer of musical instruments in Greenwich Village, New York City:

I used to go to D'Angelico's shop when I was in high school. It was just on the edge of Little Italy, south and east of the West Village. He was a wonderful man; he looked like the neighborhood butcher. If he liked you he'd give you the world; if he didn't he'd be cordial but when you left he'd say, "I'll put your fish in your guitar."

I've seen several hundred D'Angelicos and D'Aquistos—every one a masterpiece. You either have the emotional involvement with this kind of thing or you don't. Jimmy D'Aquisto had it in spades. He was not only the master of his day, but one of the world's great makers like the old man was.

D'Aquistos have a different sound than D'Angelicos. I have been trying to quantify that in my mind for years. I know what the difference is, but I can't pinpoint it verbally; its sort of like describing two different types of apples. If I had to describe the tone in simple terms I think the best description would be "smooth and clear."

Prices have gone up more in the last years. When I began to get them they sold for around $1,000 to $1,500, and now they go for $7,000 and up.

There is absolutely nobody in the category of D'Angelico and D'Aquisto as far as carved-top guitars go.

Guitarist Billy Bauer played in Woody Herman's First Herd swing-era big band:

My guitar is a 17-inch Excel, #1933, and it has an extra-wide fingerboard. When the guitar was finished [in 1954] John told me to come down to the shop at about 5:00 P.M. When I arrived he locked the front door and took me in the back room. He opened a bottle of Gallo wine, got the guitar, and said, "Play

Billy Bauer with his D'Angelico Excel. Note the zero fret.
(Photo courtesy of Billy Bauer.)

my guitar." We finished the bottle. There is an inlaid star on the back of the head, and in 1985 Jimmy D'Aquisto restored the guitar (including refinishing).

Stan Jay is the owner of the Mandolin Brothers instrument shop on Staten Island, long known as a knowledgeable source for vintage stringed instruments internationally. Mr. Jay noted the following:

> In the pantheon of twentieth-century guitar makers no one occupies a more exalted position than John D'Angelico. His guitars regularly command among the highest prices on the vintage market because of their rarity, their distinctive melodious tone and tremendous volume, the beauty of their design, and their unsurpassed level of craftsmanship.
>
> Jimmy D'Aquisto could have been content just to be the heir apparent to John's legacy but he wasn't satisfied to simply make more D'Angelico-style guitars. The changes, at first, came about slowly, but by the end of his career his designs were truly his own and were at the avant garde of modern arch-top building (which was convenient because one of his models was the "Avant Garde"). These late models, also exemplified by the Solo and the Centura, did more than just please (and enrich) their purchasers, they actually redefined what an arch-top guitar can be. This one man literally changed the course of modern guitar design.
>
> Where do we see the works and the influence of John D'Angelico and Jimmy D'Aquisto in the future? We see their bequest living on through the effect that their pioneering efforts had on builders of today and into the next century. We see the prices of their guitars continuing to appreciate substantially as new generations discover the pleasure of owning some of the most majestic musical instruments ever made. More than just being inanimate objects made of maple, spruce, ebony, pearl and steel, the products of these men's lives bridges the distance between craft and art, commerce and music.

Headpiece of the D'Aquisto 25th Anniversary New Yorker built in 1989 (#1211).
(Photo by Paul Gudelsky; courtesy of the Guild of American Luthiers.)

For the better part of twenty years, Jimmy D'Aquisto had his instruments photographed by Joshua McClure of Island Color Photo in Saint James, New York. D'Aquisto sent these photos to prospective customers, and many have appeared in magazines. D'Aquisto never informed Mr. McClure of the serial numbers of the instruments that were photographed, so the following instruments appear without their dates or serial numbers noted. Nonetheless, this gallery represents one of the most complete collections of D'Aquisto instruments photographed in a professional setting.

D'Aquisto Advance—the latest model before his death. Note the sound hole cover feature. *(Photo by Joshua McClure/Island Color Photo; from the Chinery Collection.)*

Detail of the D'Aquisto Advance. *(Photo by Joshua McClure/Island Color Photo; from the Chinery Collection.)*

Avant Garde. *(Photo by Joshua McClure/Island Color Photo.)*

Solo. *(Photo by Joshua McClure/Island Color Photo.)*

Centura. *(Photo by Joshua McClure/Island Color Photo.)*

Centura solid body. *(Photo by Joshua McClure/Island Color Photo.)*

A solid body from the 1990s. *(Photo by Joshua McClure/Island Color Photo.)*

An oval-hole New Yorker Classic. *(Photo by Joshua McClure/Island Color Photo.)*

The one-of-a-kind D'Aquisto with added fin (a design taken from a similarly constructed D'Angelico). *(Photo by Joshua McClure/Island Color Photo; from the Chinery Collection.)*

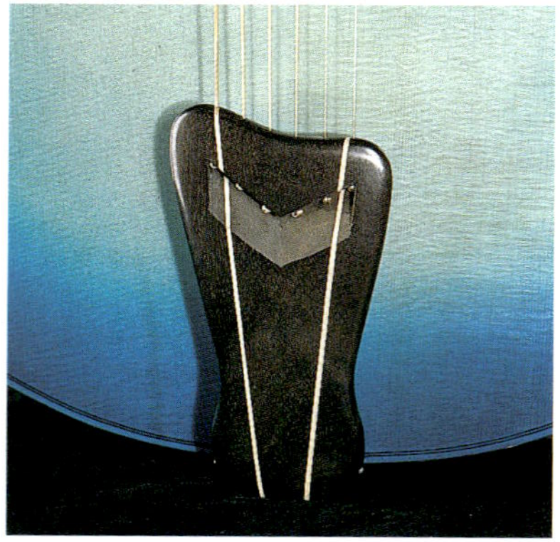

Full front view, body detail, tailpiece, and headpiece of the D'Aquisto Centura Deluxe. (*All photos by Joshua McClure/Island Color Photo; from the Chinery Collection.*)

A classic twelve-string, perhaps the first D'Aquisto with "classic" cosmetics (left). A flat-top, circa early 1980s (middle). A plywood instrument circa 1980 (right). (All photos by Joshua McClure/Island Color Photo.)

A 1980s twelve-string Excel headpiece. *(Photo by Joshua McClure/Island Color Photo.)*

A 1990s twelve-string incarnation. *(Photo by Joshua McClure/Island Color Photo.)*

Bridge detail of Solo. *(Photo by Joshua McClure/Island Color Photo.)*

D'Aquisto 25th Anniversary New Yorker (#1211) (17 inches). *(Photo by Robert Desmond and courtesy of the Guild of American Luthiers; special thanks to the Bob Mattingly Memorial Fund.)*

D'Aquisto Excel, 1970. *(Photo by Robert Desmond and courtesy of the Guild of American Luthiers; special thanks to the Bob Mattingly Memorial Fund.)*

D'Angelico plywood Electric #101 (his first of this model) of 1966. *(Photo courtesy of Dick Boak.)*

Detail of Electric #101.

D'Aquisto Centura #1256, the last model entry in D'Aquisto's ledger. The bridge, nut, and truss rod cover were completed by John Monteleone. This guitar was one of D'Aquisto's last gifts to us. *(Photo by Jose Gaytan; courtesy of Perry Beekman.)*

D'Aquisto bending sides in his shop (left). Sides in a form (right). *(Both photos by Joshua McClure/Island Color Photo.)*

D'Aquisto playing one of his Excel instruments. *(Photo by Joshua McClure/Island Color Photo.)*

George Gruhn is the founder of Gruhn Guitars in Nashville and is recognized as an authority on vintage instruments:

> Freddie Rundquist of Chicago [a studio guitar player and frequent performer] was one of the ones that really introduced me to D'Angelico instruments; I really knew very little before Freddie. There was a reputation among those that really knew what was going on that the D'Angelico was a great guitar. They were clearly better than Gibsons and Epiphones, for those that knew the difference. D'Angelico had fine quality wood, and though the tops and backs were carefully graduated, they were quite thick. They don't always tend to be very lively, but they are well balanced. There are some that are thinner and I personally like those better. D'Aquistos were much thinner and livelier.
>
> D'Angelicos and D'Aquistos vary greatly because the things they were trying to build into their instruments varied from customer to customer. They have a characteristic sound, but it is so tailored. D'Aquisto was more of a custom builder; he spoke with his customers about what they were trying to achieve. I think D'Aquisto's workmanship was neater and cleaner than D'Angelico's ever was—often D'Angelico's workmanship was sloppy. But sloppy workmanship and quality of sound don't necessarily relate. If you have great workmanship and wonderful materials and a lousy design you will have a rotten instrument. Both D'Angelico and D'Aquisto instruments are very well designed. D'Angelicos are as strong as can be, about as trouble-free as any acoustic guitars have ever been. Each maker has a signature sound, and the persons buying these instruments are doing so for their acoustic properties.
>
> I never did see very many through the store, possibly three a year. They are not fad-oriented guitars at all. They have steadily increased in value over the years and it appears as though they will continue to do so.

Larry Wexer has an M.A. in Ethnomusicology and Folklore from Indiana University and has published numerous articles on vintage guitars and mandolins. He is also an independent vintage instrument broker and professional musician and has had copious experience with some of the finest arch-top guitars ever produced:

> I love the guitars made by D'Angelico and D'Aquisto; however, there is tremendous variation in their output. D'Angelico guitars were made for a tremendous range of guitar players. He made plain and fancy guitars for people of both modest and affluent means. Some D'Angelicos are great and some are not so great. No one bats 1.000. Yet the overall standard remains very high. The workmanship ranges from a bit free and sloppy to remarkably precise. The later period, when Jimmy was helping a great deal with the guitars, shows the greatest precision and cleanest work. Some were made as rhythm guitars and are not as responsive for modern "sensitive"-style playing as are the guitars he made for leading modern jazz players. These instruments, X-braced cutaway guitars, have set the pattern for all arch-top guitars that have followed. The best of these guitars are the best ever made except possibly for the guitars of his star apprentice James D'Aquisto.
>
> I personally prefer Jimmy's mature middle-period instruments, especially those made in the 1980s. The early D'Aquistos were very much like the late D'Angelicos. Soon Jimmy began to find his own voice in the guitars; they have a smoother sound and the instruments are more responsive to a light touch. The added sensitivity of these guitars is what makes them incredibly versatile for the "modern player" who plays finger-style chord melody, as well as lines and rhythm. I feel his guitars from the 1980s have the punch and cutting power of traditional arch-tops with an added warmth of sound; what he referred to as a more "flat-top-like" sound. He continued to pursue this type of tone in his modern guitars like the New Yorker Classic, Avant Garde, Solo, and Centura, but these guitars to me lose a bit of the punch of the earlier ones. The late modernistic guitars show great vision and daring in their architecture. The Solo is one of the most visually striking designs made by any guitar maker.

David Sebring is a professional musician and arch-top specialist and served in the capacity of the latter for the better part of a quarter of a century at Gruhn Guitars in Nashville. Mr. Sebring has been a professional guitarist since 1965 and is one of the most experienced and articulate authorities on acoustic arch-top guitars in the world:

> I have had the good fortune of playing many D'As over the years in many settings, from recording studios to live gigs, and the balance of the D'Angelico guitar with its large warm notes and its complexity of permeating tone, along with its great dynamic ability always made me feel sure-footed in any musical situation—even regal. I'm at home on any arch-top instrument, toughing out their more physically demanding attack and coaxing out a thick woody tone (trying to emulate my hero Eddie Lang), but there is nothing quite like a D'A.
>
> The first D'A I ever purchased was in the early 1970s from a wise old collector who told me, "Dave, this will be quite valuable some day." I was so worried about owning it that I returned it a few days later!
>
> I recall one gig at the New Orleans Jazz and Heritage Festival when the sound of my old '34 D'Angelico Excel brought one veteran New Orleans jazz trumpeter to pat my guitar after each set and exclaim, "I haven't heard this sound in years!" He disappeared into the 3 A.M. fog at Jackson Square with a Scotch in one hand and a beautifully engraved trumpet in the other—that was a good gig.
>
> One time I left my Excel outside in a parking lot in Nashville after a gig and didn't notice it wasn't in the back seat until after I got home. I raced back to the parking lot at 90 mph only to find the D'Angelico defending its parking space with some undefinable aura! I kissed the ground. After that scare, when I played gigs I even took the Excel with me to the restroom on breaks, which always made the waiters laugh.
>
> These guitars just seem to harmonize with themselves—so in tune, so floating, so "of the angels." Thank you John. Thank you.

Last, and perhaps least, I offer a few words on my personal encounter with these men and their works. When I began this project in 1981, the arch-top guitar was relatively inconspicuous and certainly not popular. Jimmy D'Aquisto had a waiting list, but his instruments were primarily known to the jazz community. I felt these guitars were underappreciated and certainly under-utilized as acoustic instruments. My enthusiasm for them emanated from how stupendously they functioned musically (and of course their visual "swoon-factor" as well). I was fortunate enough to own and write and record my first four albums with D'As, and I loved them for all of the ideas they gave me and the sounds which so often thrilled me. I wanted to share that experience, the instruments, and their creators in hopes that others might enjoy the same—hence the idea for this book took on more and more meaning as the years progressed. As D'Angelicos and D'Aquistos became more popular, especially in the late 1990s, they did receive the recognition they were due, but the liability of that situation was that they were distanced from many players, due to their cost.

As time passed, though I always admired the instruments, I became more interested in Jimmy than in his guitars. I have fond memories of long discussions about art and creating—places where we connected. When I heard about his death it was a terrible moment—shocking, the way the death of a loved one always is. I miss him. But of course my sadness bears testament to what a wonderful thing it was to have known him. He was a complex fellow and he had his moments, like we all do, but his was an impassioned spirit—both in fervour and in gentleness.

I hope you found the book of some use to you; and remember: the most important thing about any guitar is the person playing it.

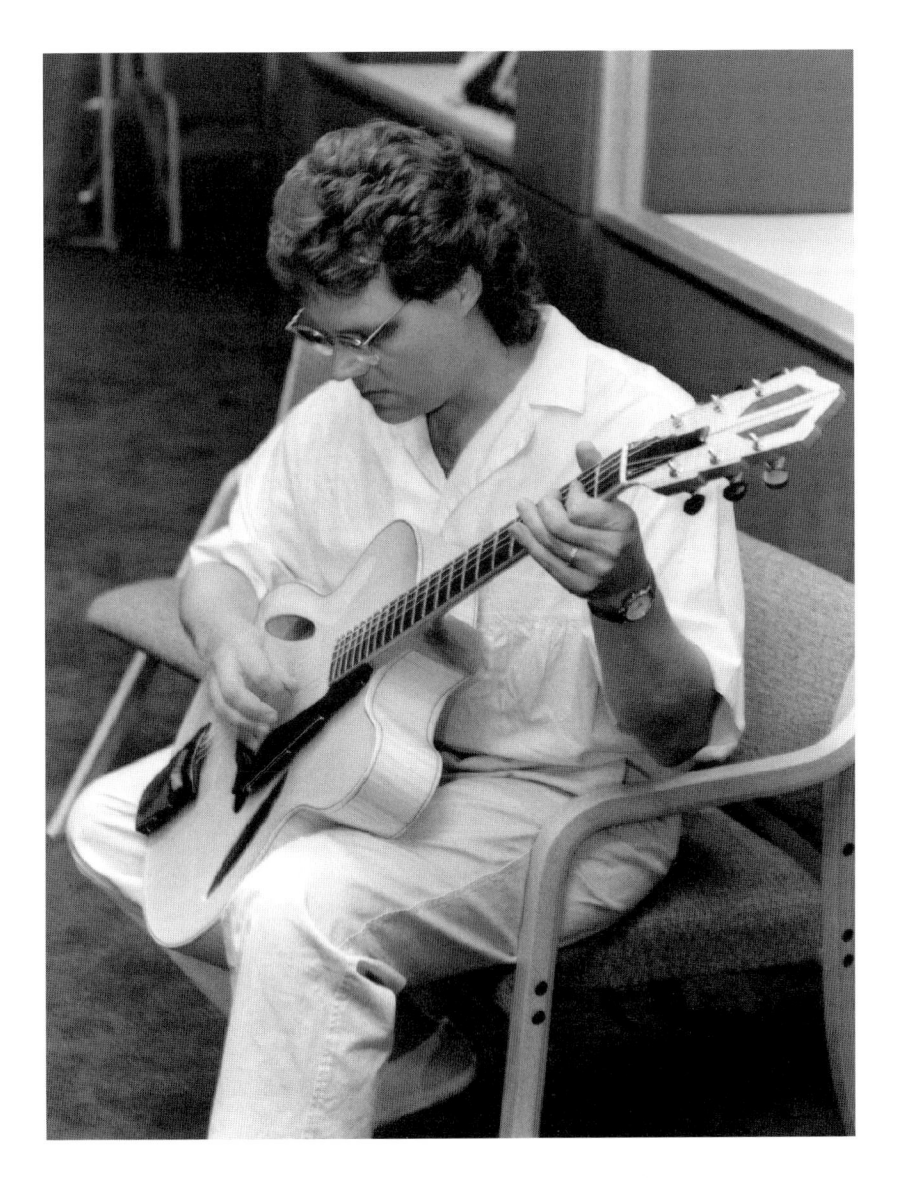

The author playing a D'Aquisto Avant Garde at the Guild of American Luthiers convention in 1995). *(Photo courtesy of Robert Desmond.)*

APPENDIXES

The Ledgers

What follows are transcriptions of the ledger books kept by John D'Angelico and James L. D'Aquisto. These are included here for reference purposes, although they do include inaccuracies.

In the original books, there are places where the writing has been smudged (or has deteriorated), where numbers and dates and words are written over each other, and where arrows are drawn from one entry to another. The reader will also notice what appear to be typographical errors and omissions, but the absence of a date or model and the occasional repetition of numbers is as the books depict. Obviously D'Angelico and D'Aquisto did not keep these books so a scholar could reconstruct an accounting of their creations. Yet, in spite of these idiosyncrasies, the ledgers represent the most comprehensive list of D'Angelico and D'Aquisto instruments.

The dates in the D'Angelico ledgers indicate when an instrument was completed or, possibly, shipped. The D'Aquisto ledgers note the date when an instrument was completed, which is not to be confused with the date found on the inside back of the instrument, which indicates the date of the completion of the back only. When a date is obviously incorrect; it has been corrected.

The reader will also notice the frequent use of the term "Special," particularly in the D'Angelico ledger. There is no way of determining exactly what the term implies, though it seems to indicate some distinct model variation. D'Angelico had several designations for what has come to be known as the New Yorker

Special, the term D'Aquisto standardized for a 17-inch instrument with New Yorker cosmetic features. The terms Small New Yorker, Excel 1000, New Yorker Special 1000, Excel Johnnie Smith (note the consistent misspelling of "Johnny"), and even Excel New Yorker are all synonymous. It seems that in earlier days the distinction between the Excel and New Yorker was in the body size, but, as customers requested the New Yorker cosmetic package on a 17-inch instrument, the terms became interchangeable.

A Mel Bay is D'Angelico's name for an 18-inch New Yorker. D'Aquisto called an 18-inch New Yorker a New Yorker Deluxe. D'Aquisto coined the name Jim Hall Model for an instrument with a type of finish in which the shading is left covering the trim.

Some of the D'Angelico entries are labeled "O"; it is not clear whether this was intended to indicate a round-hole or an oval-hole instrument. D'Aquisto recalled that many of the D'Angelicos with a single sound hole were round-hole instruments. Twice (nos. 1741 and 1742) D'Angelico's ledger notes the use of "hardened steel and spring"; this is a reference to the truss rod configuration. Until 1957, D'Angelico also logged which instruments were cutaways; after that, the feature became the norm and was no longer listed.

Although the ledgers record the person or business to whom each instrument was sold, I have elected to delete that portion in my transcription for the sake of privacy.

D'Angelico Ledger

Number	Model	Date
LOOSE SHEET		
1002	—	11/28/32
1006	—	11/21/32
1007	—	11/21/32
1020	—	10/20/32
1022	—	5/25/33
1024	left-handed	7/10/33
1032	Style-B	9/2/33
1034	—	9/2/33
1041	—	4/30/34
1042	—	12/2/33
1044	—	12/29/33
1045	tenor guitar	—
1047	Style-B	—
1048	Style-B	—
1061	—	4/10/34
1062	—	5/4/34
1063	—	3/31/34
1067	—	5/23/34
1069	—	4/30/34
1070	—	4/7/34
1071	—	6/2/34
1072	—	6/2/34
1073	—	7/20/34
1086	—	11/6/33
1091	Excel	—

Number	Model	Date
BOOK ONE		
1097	Excel	—
1105	Excel	—
1129	Excel	—
1138	Excel	—
1169	Style-B	1/36
1170	Excel	3/16/36
1171	Excel	3/10/36
1172	Style-A	3/10/36
1173	Excel	3/18/36
1174	Style-B	3/10/36
1180	Excel	4/13/36
1181	Excel	4/10/36
1182	Style-B	4/22/36
1183	Excel	4/15/36
1184	Excel	5/15/36
1185	Excel	5/11/36
1186	Excel	5/1/36
1187	Special	5/18/36
1188	Special	5/18/36
1189	Excel	5/23/36
1190	Excel	6/6/36
1191	Excel	6/12/36
1192	Excel	6/12/36
1193	Excel	6/20/36
1194	Style-B	6/20/36

Number	Model	Date	Number	Model	Date
1195	Special	7/3/36	1232	Excel	12/8/36
1196	Special	7/3/36	1233	Excel	12/29/36
1197	Style-B	7/9/36	1234	Style-B	1/20/37
1198	Style-A	7/11/36	1235	Excel	12/19/36
1199	Style-A	7/11/36	1236	Style-B	1/8/37
1200	tenor guitar	7/14/36	1237	Excel	1/37
1201	Excel	8/15/36	1238	Excel	2/11/37
1202	Excel	8/7/36	1239	Excel	—
1203	Special	7/18/36	1240	Excel	—
1204	Special	8/8/36	1241	Excel	2/19/37
1205	Special	8/12/36	1242	New Yorker	2/15/37
1206	Style-B	8/21/36	1243	Style-A	2/11/37
1207	Excel	8/23/36	1244	Tenor	2/11/37
1208	New Yorker	9/26/36	1245	Style-B	2/27/37
1209	Special	9/10/36	1246	Style-B	2/22/37
1210	Style-A	9/4/36	1247	New Yorker	3/25/37
1211	Excel	10/10/36	1248	Excel	3/20/37
1212	—	—	1249	Excel	3/13/37
1213	Excel	9/15/36	1250	Style-A	3/37
1214	Excel	9/21/36	1251	Style-B	3/17/37
1215	Tenor Style-B	9/22/36	1252	Style-B	3/25/37
1216	Special	10/10/36	1253	New Yorker	3/25/37
1217	Style-A	10/24/36	1254	Style-A	4/37
1218	Style-B	10/21/36	1255	Style-A	4/37
1219	Style-B	10/29/36	1256	Style-A	4/37
1220	Special	10/13/36	1257	Excel	—
1221	Excel	11/2/36	1258	Excel	4/22/37
1222	Excel	10/13/36	1259	Excel	5/37
1223	Excel	11/12/36	1260	Excel	5/37
1224	Excel	10/23/36	1261	New Yorker	5/37
1225	A-1	—	1262	Excel	5/37
1226	Style-A	11/11/36	1263	New Yorker	5/37
1227	Style-A	11/25/36	1264	Style-A	5/37
1228	—	—	1265	Style-A	5/37
1229	Style-A	12/5/36	1266	Style-B	6/3/37
1230	New Yorker	12/12/36	1267	Special	6/12/37
1231	Style-B	12/14/36	1268	Style-B	6/19/37

Number	Model	Date	Number	Model	Date
1269	Excel	6/12/37	1306	Style-B	11/24/37
1270	Style-B	6/26/37	1307	Style-B	11/24/37
1271	New Yorker	7/26/37	1308	Excel	11/23/37
1272	New Yorker	7/3/37	1309	Excel Tenor	12/28/37
1273	Excel	7/2/37	1310	E	—
1274	Excel	7/7/37	1311	Excel	12/9/37
1275	Style-A	7/26/37	1312	Excel	12/10/37
1276	Style-A	7/6/37	1313	Special	12/14/37
1277	Style-B	7/23/37	1314	Special	1/2/38
1278	Style-B	7/30/37	1315	Excel	12/28/37
1279	Style-A	7/30/37	1316	Excel	12/17/37
1280	Style-A	8/21/37	1317	Style-B	12/18/37
1281	Style-A	8/23/37	1318	Style-A	1/31/38
1282	Excel	8/4/37	1319	Excel	1/10/38
1283	Excel	8/21/37	1320	Excel	1/28/38
1284	Excel	8/20/37	1321	New Yorker	1/22/38
1285	New Yorker	9/21/37	1322	New Yorker	1/31/38
1286	Style-B	9/28/37	1323	Special 100	2/18/38
1287	Style-B	10/1/37	1324	Special 100	2/18/38
1288	Excel	9/22/37	1325	New Yorker	2/26/38
1289	New Yorker	9/22/37	1326	Special New Yorker	2/28/38
1290	Style-A	9/27/37	1327	Excel	2/18/38
1291	Style-B	9/25/37	1328	Style-A	2/28/38
1292	Style-A	9/28/37	1329	—	—
1293	Excel	10/28/37	1330	Excel	3/2/38
1294	New Yorker	10/23/37	1331	—	—
1295	New Yorker	10/5/37	1332	New Yorker	3/26/38
1296	New Yorker	10/16/37	1333	New Yorker	3/26/38
1297	Style-A	10/15/37	1334	Style-B	3/26/38
1298	Style-B	10/28/37	1335	Style-A	3/29/38
1299	Style-A	10/23/37	1336	Excel	3/31/38
1300	Excel Special	10/23/37	1337	Style-B	—
1301	New Yorker	—	1338	—	—
1302	New Yorker	—	1339	—	—
1303	Excel	11/10/37	1340	New Yorker	5/11/38
1304	Style-A	11/23/37	1341	A-1	5/2/38
1305	Excel	11/14/37	1342	A-1	6/7/38

160 APPENDIXES

Number	Model	Date
1343	Style-B	5/9/38
1344	Excel	5/27/38
1345	New Yorker	5/20/38
1346	Excel	5/24/38
1347	Excel	6/23/38
1348	B	7/14/38
1349	New Yorker	6/23/38
1350	B	7/8/38
1351	A-1	6/16/38
1352	A	7/6/38
1353	Excel	6/21/38
1354	A-1	6/17/38
1355	New Yorker	6/18/38
1356	Excel	7/14/38
1357	Excel	8/3/38
1358	Style-A	8/3/38
1359	Excel	8/2/38
1360	A-1	8/11/38
1361	A-1	8/31/38
1362	New Yorker	—
1363	Excel	8/13/38
1364	Excel	8/23/38
1365	Excel	12/31/38
1366	Excel	—
1367	A-1	—
1368	Style-A	9/10/38
1369	A-1	10/13/38
1370	New Yorker	1/21/39
1371	A-1	10/15/38
1372	Style-B	12/1/38
1373	Style-B	11/15/38
1374	—	—
1375	Special Large Guitar	11/28/38
1376	Excel	—
1376	New Yorker	12/7/38
1378	Style-A	12/19/38
1379	Excel	11/29/38

Number	Model	Date
1380	Excel	12/8/38
1381	Style-B	12/3/38
1382	A-1	12/7/38
1383	A-1	12/15/38
1384	Special	12/21/38
1385	A-1	12/19/38
1386	—	—
1387	—	—
1388	Excel	1/11/39
1389	Style-B	1/24/39
1390	Style-A	1/4/39
1391	A	1/26/39
1392	A	1/26/39
1393	A-1	2/4/39
1394	New Yorker	2/16/39
1395	New Yorker	2/16/39
1396	Style-A	2/2/39
1397	A-1	2/16/39
1398	Style-A	3/15/39
1399	Style-A-1	4/1/39
1400	Special	3/15/39
1401	Style-A	3/14/39
1402	—	3/31/39
1403	New Yorker	3/6/39
1404	New Yorker	—
1405	Style-B	3/31/39
1406	Style-B	4/1/39
1407	Special Large	—
1408	Style-A	—
1409	Style-A-1	—
1410	Special Large	4/25/39
1411	New Yorker	5/27/39
1412	A-1	5/5/39
1413	Special Large	5/8/39
1414	A-1	—
1415	Excel	5/23/39
1416	Style-B	5/20/39

D'ANGELICO LEDGER

Number	Model	Date
1417	A-1	6/5/39
1418	Special Large	6/10/39
1419	Style-A	6/17/39
1420	A	6/17/39
1420	Excel	7/8/39
1421	+ Special	7/3/39
1422	A-1	6/29/39
1423	+ Special	7/8/39
1424	Style-B	7/1/39
1425	Special New Yorker	7/15/39
1426	A-1	7/18/39
1427	Style-A	7/19/39
1428	New Yorker	8/15/39
1429	Special	8/29/39
1430	Excel	8/4/39
1431	Style-B	8/4/39
1432	Style-B	8/3/39
1433	Style-A	8/25/39
1434	Style-A	10/7/39
1435	Style-A	9/5/39
1436	B-Special	9/21/39
1437	B-Special	9/39
1438	A-1	9/25/39
1439	Excel	10/16/39
1440	V.A. Special	10/18/39
1441	Style-B	10/17/39
1442	A-1	10/17/39
1443	A-1	10/17/39
1444	New Yorker	10/30/39
1445	Excel	11/11/39
1446	Excel	11/13/39
1447	Style-A	11/11/39
1448	Special Large	1/6/40
1449	Style-B	11/25/39
1450	Style-B	11/22/39
1451	Style-B	11/30/39
1452	A-1	12/2/39

Number	Model	Date
1453	A-1	10/39
1454	Style-B	10/39
1455	A-1	12/9/39
1456	Style A-1	12/30/39
1457	A-1	1/11/40
1458	A-1	1/22/40
1459	Style-A	2/1/40
1460	Style-A	2/26/40
1461	A-1	2/22/40
1462	Style-B	2/19/40
1463	New Yorker	2/19/40
1464	Style-B	2/27/40
1465	Special	3/26/40
1466	Special, Natural Finish	3/23/40
1467	Style-B	3/2/40
1468	Excel	4/12/40
1469	New Yorker	3/16/40
1470	Style-A	3/31/40
1471	Special, Natural Finish	3/23/40
1472	A-1	4/1/40
1473	Large Special, White A-1	4/15/40
1474	Excel	4/19/40
1475	Tenor Excel	5/16/40
1476	New Yorker	7/18/40
1477	Style-B	6/40
1478	New Yorker	6/5/40
1479	Special	6/1/40
1480	Style-B, O	6/10/40
1481	Excel	6/14/40
1482	Excel	7/24/40
1483	Excel	6/25/40
1484	A-1	6/15/40
1485	Style-A	6/11/40
1486	Style-A	7/17/40
1487	Style-A	7/11/40
1488	Excel	7/22/40

162 APPENDIXES

Number	Model	Date
1489	New Yorker	8/20/40
1490	New Yorker	7/20/40
1491	A-1	8/3/40
1492	Special	8/10/40
1493	A-1	8/17/40
1494	Style-A	9/9/40
1495	New Yorker	11/2/40
1496	New Yorker	9/1/40
1497	A-1	9/21/40
1498	Special Large	9/25/40
1499	Special	10/26/40
1500	Special, Birdseye	10/28/40
1501	Style-A	10/40
1502	A-1	10/23/40
1503	Excel	11/2/40
1504	Style-A	11/2/40
1505	Special	11/16/40
1506	Style-B	11/29/40
1507	A-1	11/30/40
1507	Style-B	12/28/40
1508	Style-A	12/28/40
1509	Excel	1/3/41
1510	Style-A	1/19/41
1511	Excel, Stripe	4/8/41
1512	Excel	3/31/41
1513	New Yorker	2/11/41
1514	New Yorker	3/17/41
1515	Special	2/11/41
1516	A-1 Special	2/20/41
1517	A-1	3/8/41
1518	A-1	3/15/41
1519	Style-A	3/22/41
1520	New Yorker	4/8/40
1521	A-1	4/9/41
1522	A-1	4/25/41
1523	A-1	4/25/41
1523	Excel	—

Number	Model	Date
1524	New Yorker	5/3/41
1525	Large Special	5/21/41
1526	Excel	7/19/41
1527	A-1	6/28/41
1528	Style-B	6/10/41
1529	Special	6/12/41
1530	New Yorker	6/7/41
1531	A-1	6/21/41
1532	A-1	5/21/41
1533	Excel	6/28/41
1534	Special	7/1/41
1535	A-1	7/21/41
1536	A-1	7/28/41
1537	Excel	9/20/41
1538	Excel	8/12/41
1539	A-1	8/6/41
1540	Style-B	8/26/41
1541	A-1	9/6/41
1542	Excel	9/9/41
1543	Style-A	9/9/41
1544	Excel	9/2/41
1545	A-1	9/22/41
1546	A-1	9/23/41
1547	Special	10/1/41
1548	Style-A	4/6/42
1549	A-1	10/11/41
1550	Style-B	10/18/41
1551	Special	10/22/41
1552	Excel	10/20/41
1553	Excel	10/28/41
1554	A-1	10/24/41
1555	A-1	10/28/41
1556	A-1	10/28/41
1557	Excel	11/18/41
1558	Excel	11/17/41
1559	Excel	12/13/41
1560	Excel	12/16/41

Number	Model	Date	Number	Model	Date
1561	Excel	12/6/41	1598	Excel	7/22/42
1562	Excel	12/7/41	1599	Excel	10/24/42
1563	New Yorker	1/22/42	1600	A-1	8/42
1564	New Yorker	1/14/42	1601	A-1	8/42
1565	A-1	8/1/42	1602	New Yorker	9/25/42
1566	Style-A	1/12/42	1603	Excel	11/42
1567	A-1	11/23/42	1604	Special	8/20/42
1568	Excel	5/20/42	1604	Tenor Guitar	8/29/42
1569	A-1	2/17/42	1605	A-1	9/10/42
1570	Special	2/10/42	1606	Style-A	9/42
1571	New Yorker	2/1/42	1607	A-]	10/10/42
1572	Special	2/2/42	1608	Style-A	11/1/42
1573	Style-A	2/14/42	1609	Excel	10/8/42
1574	A-1	2/16/42	1610	New Yorker	10/24/42
1575	Special	2/24/42	1611	Excel	10/26/42
1576	Special	2/24/42	1612	A-1	10/31/42
1577	Excel	3/3/42	1613	A-1	11/21/42
1578	Special	3/17/42	1614	Excel	11/28/42
1579	A-1	3/23/42	1615	Style-B	11/28/42
1580	A-1	3/27/42	1616	Excel	11/28/42
1581	Style-B	3/27/42	1617	A-1	12/16/42
1582	Excel	4/4/42	1618	A-1	12/22/42
1583	New Yorker	5/27/42	1619	A-1	12/28/42
1584	A-1	6/1/42	1620	Excel	12/26/42
1585	Excel	4/27/42	1621	New Yorker	12/26/42
1586	A-1	5/23/42	1622	Style-B	1/43
1587	A-1	5/22/42	1623	Excel	2/5/43
1588	Excel	6/3/42	1624	New Yorker	2/43
1589	Style-B	5/11/42	1625	A-1	2/9/43
1590	Special	5/15/42	1626	Excel	2/3/43
1591	Style-A	6/10/42	1627	Style-A	3/6/43
1592	Excel	7/21/42	1628	Excel	3/9/43
1593	Style-A	6/18/42	1629	A-1	3/15/43
1594	Excel	6/20/42	1630	New Yorker	4/8/43
1595	Style-A	7/23/42	1631	Excel	3/31/43
1596	A-1	7/24/42	1632	Style-B Special	4/3/43
1597	Style-A	7/28/42	1633	Style-A	4/16/43

164 APPENDIXES

Number	Model	Date
1634	Excel	5/3/43
1635	Special A	5/8/43
1636	Excel	5/13/43
1637	Excel	5/24/43
1638	New Yorker	5/29/43
1639	Style-B	7/6/43
1640	Style-A	6/22/43
1641	Excel	7/3/43
1642	Style-A	7/27/43
1643	B Special	8/3/43
1644	Style-A	8/2/43
1645	Excel	8/12/43
1646	New Yorker	8/24/43
1647	Excel	9/4/43
1648	Style-A	9/7/43
1649	New Yorker	9/18/43
1650	Style-A	10/11/43
1651	Style-A	10/9/43
1652	A-1	10/19/43
1653	Tenor Excel	10/11/43
1654	Excel	10/11/43
1655	New Yorker	11/29/43
1656	Style-A	11/8/43
1657	Style-A	11/1/43
1658	Small New Yorker	11/19/43
1659	Excel	11/16/43
1660	Style-B	11/10/43
1661	A-1	11/20/43
1662	Style-A	11/25/43
1663	Excel	12/29/43
1664	Style-A	1/7/44
1665	Excel	1/22/44
1666	Excel	1/26/44
1667	Style-A	2/22/44
1668	Excel	2/25/44
1669	New Yorker	—
1670	Excel	3/7/44

Number	Model	Date
1671	Style-A	4/1/44
1672	Style-A	4/10/44
1673	Excel	3/30/44
1674	Excel	5/27/44
1675	Special	5/13/44
1676	New Yorker	6/44
1677	Excel	8/7/44
1678	Excel	8/7/44
1679	Excel	11/14/44
1680	Excel	1/6/45
1681	New Yorker	12/30/44
1682	Style-A	1/6/45
1683	Excel	1/19/45
1684	New Yorker	2/3/45
1685	Excel	4/45
1686	Excel	9/6/45
1687	New Yorker	5/5/45
1687	Excel	5/21/45
1688	Excel	7/18/45
1689	Excel	8/6/45
1690	Style-A	9/14/45
1691	Excel	10/4/45
1692	New Yorker	10/10/45
1693	Excel	10/20/45
1694	Style-B	12/4/45
1695	Tenor	12/8/45
1696	Excel	12/7/45
1697	Excel	12/19/45
1698	New Yorker	12/45
1699	Excel	—
1700	Excel	—
1701	Excel	—
1702	New Yorker	3/46
1703	Excel	4/19/46
1704	Excel	4/15/46
1705	Excel	4/13/46
1706	Excel	5/1/46

Number	Model	Date
1707	—	—
1708	New Yorker	5/10/46
1709	New Yorker	5/25/46
1710	Excel	5/14/46
1711	Excel	5/18/46
1712	New Yorker	6/7/46
1713	New Yorker	6/20/46
1714	New Yorker	6/19/46
1715	New Yorker	6/18/46
1716	Style-B	6/15/46
1717	Style-B	6/19/46
1718	Excel	7/16/46
1719	Excel	7/3/46
1720	Style-B	7/10/46
1721	Style-B	7/10/46
1722	New Yorker	8/5/46
1723	New Yorker	8/14/46
1724	New Yorker	8/20/46
1725	Excel	8/24/46
1726	New Yorker	8/29/46
1727	New Yorker	9/4/46
1728	New Yorker	9/19/46
1729	New Yorker	11/7/46
1730	Excel	11/19/46
1731	Excel	11/25/46
1732	Excel	11/16/46
1733	Excel	11/21/46
1734	Excel	12/9/46
1735	Excel	12/19/46
1736	Style-B	12/16/46
1737	Excel Tenor	12/46
1738	Excel, Left-handed	1/4/47
1739	New Yorker	12/7/46
1740	New Yorker	12/24/46
1741	Special, hardened steel and spring	2/8/47

Number	Model	Date
1742	Excel, hardened steel and spring	2/8/47
1743	Excel	2/8/47
1744	New Yorker	3/4/47
1745	Excel	3/12/47
1746	Excel	3/7/47
1747	Tenor	3/25/47
1748	Excel	4/14/47
1749	Excel	4/11/47
1750	New Yorker	4/26/47
1751	New Yorker Special	5/21/47
1752	Excel Cutaway	5/9/47
1753	Special	5/21/47
1754	New Yorker	5/9/47
1755	New Yorker	6/10/47
1756	Special	6/10/47
1757	Special	6/5/47
1758	Special	6/7/47
1759	Excel	6/10/47
1760	Excel Special	6/23/47
1761	Special	7/2/47
1762	Special	7/17/47
1763	Special, Left-handed	8/47
1764	Special	9/3/47
1765	New Yorker	8/15/47
1766	New Yorker	8/20/47
1767	New Yorker	9/2/47
1768	Excel	10/10/47
1769	Excel	10/10/47
1770	Small New Yorker Cutaway	10/18/47
1771	New Yorker	11/3/47
1772	New Yorker	11/47
1773	Excel Plectrum	11/21/47
1774	Excel	11/21/47

166 APPENDIXES

Number	Model	Date
1775	Small New Yorker Cutaway	11/26/47
1776	New Yorker, Black	12/1/47
1777	Excel Cutaway	11/19/47
1778	New Yorker	12/24/47
1779	New Yorker	12/2/47
1780	Excel	12/13/47
1781	New Yorker	12/15/47
1782	Style-B	2/17/48
1783	Excel Cutaway	12/21/48
1784	New Yorker	2/20/48
1785	Excel Cutaway	4/30/48
1786	Excel	4/8/48
1787	New Yorker	4/7/48
1788	New Yorker	6/29/48
1789	Excel Cutaway	6/5/48
1790	New Yorker	6/24/48
1791	New Yorker	6/11/48
1792	New Yorker	6/25/48
1793	Excel Cutaway	6/30/48
1794	Excel Cutaway	8/11/48
1795	Excel	9/28/48
1796	Excel	10/18/48
1797	New Yorker Cutaway	9/18/48
1798	Special	5/20/49
1799	Special	12/17/48
1800	Excel Cutaway	12/10/48
1801	Excel Cutaway	11/30/48
1802	New Yorker	11/30/48
1803	Excel	12/14/48
1804	Excel	11/29/48
1805	Special New Yorker	1/7/49
1806	Excel	1/10/49
1807	Special	1/8/49
1808	New Yorker	1/15/49
1809	New Yorker Cutaway	1/14/49
1810	Excel Cutaway	2/26/49

Number	Model	Date
1811	New Yorker Cutaway	2/25/49
1812	Excel	3/11/49
1813	Excel	4/02/49
1814	Excel Cutaway	3/28/49
1815	Special	4/23/49
1816	Special	5/7/49
1817	Excel Cutaway	7/19/49
1818	Special	4/30/49
1819	New Yorker Cutaway	5/4/49
1820	Excel	5/20/49
1821	Excel New Yorker Cutaway	6/3/49
1822	Special	6/29/49
1823	Special	8/11/49
1824	Special	9/13/49
1825	Special	9/13/49
1826	New Yorker Cutaway Left-Handed	8/31/49
1827	Excel	11/5/49
1828	New Yorker	9/17/49
1829	Excel Cutaway	10/15/49
1830	New Yorker Cutaway	10/27/49
1831	New Yorker	12/24/49
1832	Excel	1/28/50
1833	Special	10/31/50
1834	New Yorker	3/13/50
1835	Excel Cutaway	3/4/50
1836	Mel Bay	11/4/50
1837	New Yorker Cutaway	3/17/50
1838	Excel Cutaway	4/8/50
1839	Excel Cutaway Electric	6/3/50
1840	New Yorker	4/27/50
1841	New Yorker Cutaway	6/13/50
1842	Excel	6/1/50
1843	Excel	6/24/50
1844	Excel	6/24/50
1845	New Yorker Special	6/9/51

Number	Model	Date
1846	Excel Cutaway Left-Handed	9/11/50
1847	Excel	—
1848	Excel	10/20/50
1849	Excel Cutaway	11/4/50

BOOK TWO

Number	Model	Date
1850	Small New Yorker Cutaway	11/27/50
1851	New Yorker	12/18/50
1852	Excel	11/28/50
1853	Excel	12/9/50
1854	New Yorker	12/11/50
1855	Excel	12/23/50
1856	New Yorker	2/23/51
1857	New Yorker	2/19/51
1858	Special Cutaway	2/19/51
1859	Special Cutaway	2/19/51
1860	Excel Cutaway	3/2/51
1861	Excel Cutaway	12/3/51
1862	New Yorker	3/10/51
1863	Excel Cutaway	4/17/51
1864	Excel Cutaway	5/8/51
1865	Excel Cutaway	5/7/51
1866	Excel Cutaway	6/21/51
1867	Tenor Excel	6/9/51
1868	Excel Cutaway	6/16/51
1869	Special	6/8/51
1870	Excel	6/18/51
1871	Excel Cutaway	8/11/51
1872	Excel Tenor	8/6/51
1873	Special	8/11/51
1874	Special	8/12/51
1875	Excel Cutaway	10/3/51
1876	Excel Cutaway	11/1/51
1877	New Yorker Cutaway	10/16/51
1878	Excel Cutaway	12/17/51

Number	Model	Date
1879	New Yorker Cutaway	11/8/51
1880	Excel Cutaway	12/21/51
1881	Excel	11/29/51
1882	New Yorker	11/21/51
1883	New Yorker	11/21/51
1884	Special Cutaway	12/21/51
1885	Special	12/27/51
1886	Mel Bay	3/26/52
1887	Mel Bay	3/26/52
1888	Excel Cutaway	3/12/52
1889	Excel	3/14/52
1890	Excel Cutaway Electric	3/21/52
1891	New Yorker Cutaway	3/24/52
1892	Excel Cutaway	5/5/52
1893	New Yorker Cutaway	4/11/52
1894	New Yorker Cutaway	5/1/52
1895	Excel Cutaway	5/9/52
1896	Excel Cutaway	7/24/52
1897	New Yorker Cutaway	7/11/52
1898	Excel Cutaway Electric	7/1/52
1899	Excel	8/29/52
1900	New Yorker Cutaway	8/9/52
1901	Excel Cutaway	7/28/52
1902	Mel Bay	10/10/52
1903	New Yorker Cutaway	9/23/52
1904	Excel	11/21/52
1905	Excel Cutaway	11/14/52
1906	New Yorker O	11/7/52
1907	Excel	1/19/53
1908	Excel Cutaway	11/19/52
1909	New Yorker Left	12/23/52
1910	Excel Cutaway	12/13/52
1911	New Yorker	2/2/53
1912	New Yorker	2/10/53
1913	Excel Cutaway	3/5/53
1914	New Yorker Cutaway	4/18/53
1915	New Yorker	4/4/53

Number	Model	Date
1916	New Yorker	4/14/53
1917	New Yorker Cutaway O	2/20/53
1918	Excel Cutaway	6/6/53
1919	Excel Cutaway	6/5/53
1920	Excel Cutaway	6/10/53
1921	New Yorker Cutaway	6/18/53
1922	Excel Cutaway	6/5/53
1923	Excel O	7/3/53
1924	Excel Regular	7/13/53
1925	Excel Cutaway	7/13/53
1926	Excel Cutaway	7/10/53
1927	New Yorker Cutaway	7/31/53
1928	New Yorker Cutaway	8/22/53
1929	Excel Regular	9/26/53
1930	Excel Cutaway	10/16/53
1931	New Yorker Cutaway	10/10/53
1932	New Yorker Cutaway	10/20/53
1933	Excel Cutaway	1/12/54
1934	New Yorker	12/22/53
1935	Excel Cutaway	12/18/53
1936	Excel	12/5/53
1937	New Yorker Regular	1/10/54
1938	New Yorker Regular	3/1/54
1939	Excel Cutaway Built-In Electrics	3/2/54
1940	Excel Cutaway	3/2/54
1941	Special Cutaway	3/13/54
1942	Excel Cutaway	4/1/54
1943	Excel Cutaway	4/10/54
1944	New Yorker Cutaway	4/24/54
1945	New Yorker Cutaway	5/1/54
1946	Special	5/21/54
1947	Excel Cutaway	5/21/54
1948	New Yorker Cutaway	7/2/54
1949	Mel Bay	8/4/54
1950	New Yorker Cutaway	7/22/54
1951	Excel Cutaway	7/23/54
1952	Excel Cutaway	7/23/54
1953	New Yorker Cutaway	9/29/54
1954	Excel Cutaway	9/23/54
1955	New Yorker Cutaway	9/24/54
1956	Excel Regular	10/1/54
1957	Excel Cutaway	11/20/54
1958	Excel Cutaway	11/10/54
1959	New Yorker Cutaway	11/27/54
1960	Mel Bay	11/22/54
1961	O New Yorker Cutaway	6/22/55
1962	Excel Cutaway	12/22/54
1963	Excel "1000" Cutaway	1/5/55
1964	Excel Cutaway	2/3/55
1965	Excel Cutaway	3/27/55
1966	Excel Cutaway	3/12/55
1967	Excel Cutaway	5/20/55
1968	New Yorker Regular	3/20/55
1969	New Yorker Cutaway	5/5/55
1970	Excel Cutaway	4/20/55
1971	Excel Cutaway	4/28/55
1972	Special Cutaway	5/27/55
1973	Excel Cutaway	7/8/55
1974	Excel Regular	6/28/55
1975	New Yorker Cutaway	5/12/55
1976	New Yorker Cutaway	8/3/55
1977	Excel Cutaway	8/26/55
1978	Excel Roundhole	10/12/55
1979	Excel Cutaway	11/16/55
1980	Special	11/25/55
1981	Excel Cutaway	10/30/55
1982	Excel Cutaway Electric	11/10/55
1983	Excel Cutaway Electric	11/10/55
1984	Excel Cutaway Electric	11/15/55
1985	New Yorker Cutaway	12/3/55
1986	Special Cutaway	12/18/55
1987	Excel Regular	12/23/55
1988	New Yorker	12/28/55

Number	Model	Date	Number	Model	Date
1989	Excel Left-Handed	1/10/56	2023	Excel Special, Imported Woods	4/57
1990	Excel Cutaway	1/20/56	2024	Excel Special, Imported Back	5/12/57
1991	New Yorker Cutaway	1/30/56	2025	—	—
1992	Excel Cutaway Electric	2/15/56	2026	Excel	5/20/57
1993	Excel Cutaway	2/22/56	2027	Excel	5/25/57
1994	New Yorker Cutaway	3/10/56	2028	Excel	6/1/57
1995	New Yorker Cutaway	3/15/56	2029	Excel Cutaway	7/25/57
1996	New Yorker Cutaway	4/3/56	2030	Excel Cutaway	6/28/57
1997	New Yorker Cutaway	4/15/56	2031	Special Cutaway	6/26/57
1998	Excel Cutaway Electric	5/1/56	2032	Special Cutaway New Yorker	—
1999	New Yorker Cutaway	5/7/56	2033	Excel, New Yorker Trim, Special Import	7/10/57
2000	New Yorker Cutaway	5/14/56	2034	Excel	8/8/57
2001	New Yorker Cutaway	5/27/56	2035	Excel	8/3/57
2002	Excel Cutaway	6/2/56	2036	Excel	8/15/57
2003	Excel Cutaway Electric	6/15/56	2037	Excel	8/20/57
2004	Excel Cutaway Johnnie Smith	7/10/56	2038	New Yorker Mel Bay Model	11/10/57
2005	Excel Cutaway Johnnie Smith	7/25/56	2039	Excel	12/21/57
2006	Excel Cutaway	8/2/56	2040	New Yorker Mel Bay Model	12/28/57
2007	Excel Cutaway Johnnie Smith	8/15/56	2041	Excel	1/25/58
2008	New Yorker Cutaway	9/1/56	2042	Special	1/28/58
2009	Excel Cutaway	—	2043	Excel	2/28/58
2010	Excel	10/19/56	2044	Excel	2/15/58
2011	Excel	11/15/56	2045	New Yorker, Imported Wood	2/10/58
2012	Special Cutaway	11/10/56	2046	Excel, Imported Wood	2/10/58
2013	—	—	2047	New Yorker, Imported Wood	2/28/58
2014	—	—	2048	Excel	3/10/58
2015	Excel	1/3/56	2049	Excel	3/15/58
2016	New Yorker	2/12/56	2050	Special New Yorker	3/25/58
2017	Excel	1/10/56	2051	Special New Yorker	—
2018	Excel	3/3/57	2052	Excel	5/26/58
2019	Excel	3/3/57			
2020	Excel Regular	4/2/57			
2021	Excel	4/10/57			
2022	Excel	4/57			

170 APPENDIXES

Number	Model	Date
2053	Excel	—
2054	Excel Electric	6/3/58
2055	Excel	6/10/58
2056	Excel	6/25/58
2057	Excel 1000	7/23/58
2058	Excel	7/15/58
2059	Excel	7/25/58
2060	Excel 1000	8/12/58
2061	New Yorker	9/20/58
2062	Excel, Special Body	10/10/58
2063	Excel	10/20/58
2064	Excel	11/5/58
2065	New Yorker Special 1000	12/10/58
2066	Excel	—
2067	New Yorker Special	12/15/58
2067	Excel, Imported	1/1/59
2068	Excel, Imported	1/3/59
2069	Excel, Imported	1/10/59
2070	Excel, Small Imported	2/2/59
2071	Excel J.S., Imported	3/10/59
2072	Excel, Imported	4/2/59
2073	Excel	4/10/59
2074	New Yorker	4/15/59
2075	Excel	4/12/59
2076	Excel	4/20/59
2077	New Yorker	5/5/59
2078	Small New Yorker	5/12/59
2079	Excel	5/20/59
2080	Excel	5/27/59
2081	Excel	6/5/59
2082	Excel	6/20/59
2083	Excel	7/15/59
2084	New Yorker	7/25/59
2085	New Yorker	8/10/59
2086	Excel	8/14/59
2087	Excel	8/12/59

Number	Model	Date
2088	Excel	8/16/59
2089	Excel	8/25/59
2090	New Yorker	9/1/59
2091	New Yorker	9/10/59
2092	Excel Double Electric	9/30/59
2093	Excel	10/10/59
2094	Excel New Yorker	12/10/59
2095	Excel New Yorker Double Imported	12/16/59
2096	New Yorker	12/18/59
2097	Excel	12/23/59
2098	Excel New Yorker	12/30/59
2099	Excel	1/10/60
2100	New Yorker	1/15/60
2101	Excel New Yorker	1/25/60
2102	Excel	2/10/60
2103	New Yorker	3/10/60
2104	Excel	3/25/60
2105	Excel	4/5/60
2106	Excel Electric	5/8/60
2107	New Yorker	5/15/60
2108	New Yorker	5/60
2109	Excel	6/10/60
2110	Excel	6/15/60
2111	Excel	6/20/60
2112	Excel	6/30/60
2113	Excel	7/10/60
2114	Excel Tenor	7/20/60
2115	Excel	8/25/60
2116	Excel	9/2/60
2117	Excel	9/22/60
2118	New Yorker	10/10/60
2119	Excel	10/30/60
2120	New Yorker	11/15/60
2121	New Yorker	12/5/60
2122	New Yorker	12/10/60
2123	New Yorker	1/10/61

Number	Model	Date	Number	Model	Date
LOOSE SHEETS			2156	Special	—
2124	Excel	—	2157	New Yorker	—
2125	Excel	—	2158	Excel	—
2126	New Yorker	—	2159	Excel Special	—
2127	Excel	—	2160	Excel Special	—
2128	Excel	—	2161	New Yorker	—
2129	New Yorker	—	2162	New Yorker	—
2130	Excel	—	2163	Excel Left-Handed	—
2131	Excel Tenor	—	2164	New Yorker	—
2132	New Yorker	—	*O1861	Special	2/21/51
2133	Excel Special	—	O1862	Special	3/3/51
2134	Excel	—	O1863	Special	3/10/51
2135	Excel	—	O1864	Special	3/20/51
2136	Excel Special	—	O1865	Special	4/15/51
2137	New Yorker Johnnie Smith Excel	—	O1866	Special	4/28/51
2138	New Yorker	—	O1929	Xe	9/23/53
2139	—	—	O2114	—	—
2140	—	—	O2112	Excel	6/1/6/60
2141	Excel Electric	—	O2113	Excel	
2142	New Yorker	—	**2211	New Yorker	12/22//55
2143	Excel	—	2212	Excel	12/10/55
2144	New Yorker	—	2213	Excel	12/15/55
2145	Excel	—	2214	Excel	1/23/56
2146	Excel	—			
2147	New Yorker	—		[MANDOLINS]	
2148	New Yorker	—	125	Scroll	4/20/40
2149	Excel	—	126	Scroll	4/19/40
2150	Excel	—	127	Scroll	4/9/40
2151	—	—	128	Plain	4/30/40
2152	New Yorker	—	129	Plain	6/13/40
2153	New Yorker	—	130	Plain	7/2/40
2154	Excel	—	131	Plain	10/26/40
2155	Excel	—	132	Scroll	11/13/40
			133	Plain	11/30/40

*Nos. O1861–O2113 appear without explanation; quite possibly, they are round-hole instruments.
**Nos. 2211–2214 are guitars with shorter bodies.

Number	Model	Date	Number	Model	Date
134	Plain	11/25/40	152	Plain	4/14/42
135	Plain	12/21/40	153	Plain	7/14/42
136	Plain	1/4/41	154	Scroll, O	7/11/42
137	Scroll	1/21/41	155	Scroll	7/29/42
138	Plain	1/20/41	156	Plain	6/20/42
139	Plain	2/12/41	157	Plain	10/21/42
140	Plain (good)	3/5/41	158	Scroll	2/6/42
141	G.D.	5/10/41	159	Scroll	—
142	Plain	5/10/41	160	Scroll	1/25/43
143	Plain	6/16/41	161	Plain	12/14/42
144	Scroll	7/1/41	162	Plain	1/25/43
145	Plain	7/1/41	163	(good)	6/2/43
146	Scroll	7/22/41	164	—	6/28/43
147	Plain	9/25/41	165	—	6/25/43
148	Plain	11/22/41	166	(good)	11/12/43
149	Scroll	6/20/42	167	Scroll	9/11/43
150	Scroll	7/30/42	168	Scroll	1944
151	Scroll	9/25/42	174	—	1954

D'Aquisto Ledger

Number	Model	Date
1001	New Yorker	5/65
1002	Excel	8/65
1003	Excel	9/65
1004	Custom Excel	10/65
1005	Excel	12/65
1006	New Yorker	3/66
1007	Excel	4/66
1007A	Excel	4/66
1008	New Yorker	4/66
1009	New Yorker	8/66
1010	New Yorker Special	9/66
1011	New Yorker	10/66
1012	New Yorker Special	11/66
1013	New Yorker	11/66
1014	New Yorker Special	7/66
1015	New Yorker Special	1/67
1016	New Yorker Deluxe, New Design	6/67
1017	New Yorker Deluxe	6/67
1018	New Yorker Deluxe	8/67
1019	Excel	10/67
1020	Excel Deluxe New Yorker Special	10/67
1021	New Yorker Deluxe	11/67
1022	Excel Deluxe New Yorker Special	12/67
1023	New Yorker Deluxe	1/68
1024	Excel Deluxe New Yorker Special	2/68
1025	Excel	4/68
1026	New Yorker	6/24/68
1027	New Yorker Deluxe	8/12/68
1028	New Yorker Special	8/12/68
1029	Excel	11/29/68
1030	New Yorker Deluxe	1/4/69
1031	New Yorker Special	2/69
1032	New Yorker Special	6/23/69
1033	New Yorker Special	9/69
1034	New Yorker Deluxe	7/9/69
1035	New Yorker Special	11/17/69
1036	New Yorker Special	1/70
1037	New Yorker Deluxe	5/27/70
1038	New Yorker Special	7/10/70
1039	Excel Special	1/70
1040	New Yorker Deluxe	4/1/70
1041	New Yorker Deluxe	5/21/70
1042	New Yorker Deluxe	1970
1043	New Yorker Deluxe	12/10/70
1044	New Yorker Deluxe	1/8/71
1045	New Yorker Deluxe	4/12/71
1046	New Yorker Special	5/71
1047	Excel, American Wood	7/71
1048	New Yorker Special	8/71

Number	Model	Date
1049	New Yorker Special	8/5/71
1050	Oval Hole Special, 17"	1/12/71
1051	New Yorker Special	2/1/72
1052	Oval Hole Special, 17"	4/3/72
1053	Oval Hole Special, 17"	3/2/72
1054	New Yorker Deluxe	4/17/72
1055	New Yorker Deluxe	5/12/72
1056	New Yorker Special	6/14/72
1057	Excel	8/28/72
1058	New Yorker Oval Hole, 17"	9/12/72
1059	New Yorker Special	11/4/72
1060	New Yorker Deluxe	10/17/72
1061	Special Oval Hole, 15"	11/9/72
1062	New Yorker Deluxe	1/23/73
1063	New Yorker Special	12/22/72
1064	New Yorker Deluxe	2/28/73
1065	New Yorker	4/20/73
1066	New Yorker Special	5/2/73
1067	New Yorker 7-String Special	5/16/73
1068	Oval Hole	8/15/73
1069	Oval Hole	7/10/73
1070	New Yorker Special	10/2/73
1071	Special 12-String	9/20/73
1072	New Yorker Deluxe	11/15/73
1073	New Yorker Special	12/13/73
1074	New Yorker Special	1/11/74
1075	New Yorker Deluxe	2/20/74
1076	New Yorker Special	3/25/74
1077	New Yorker Deluxe	5/10/74
1078	New Yorker Special	6/10/74
1079	New Yorker Special	7/18/74
1080	New Yorker Deluxe	10/3/74
1081	New Yorker Special	8/13/74
1082	New Yorker Special	9/27/74
1083	New Yorker Special	11/14/74
1084	New Yorker Deluxe	12/26/74
1085	Excel	3/6/75
1086	New Yorker Deluxe	2/20/75
1087	New Yorker Deluxe	4/20/75
1088	Excel Oval Hole	11/30/75
1089	New Yorker Deluxe	4/30/75
1090	Special Oval Hole, 16"	5/20/75
1091	Excel	6/18/75
1092	New Yorker Special, 7-String	7/25/75
1093	New Yorker Special, 7-String	8/18/75
1094	New Yorker Deluxe	9/20/75
1095	New Yorker Oval Hole, 18"	3/24/76
1096	New Yorker Deluxe	1/20/76
1097	New Yorker Special	4/28/76
1098	New Yorker Deluxe	2/24/76
1099	New Yorker Deluxe	7/11/76
1100	New Yorker Deluxe	8/19/76
1101	New Yorker Deluxe	9/30/76
1102	New Yorker Special	11/22/76
1103	New Yorker Special	1/28/77
1104	New Yorker Special	2/17/77
1105	New Yorker Deluxe	12/25/76
1106	New Yorker Special	4/2/77
1107	New Yorker Special	6/18/77
1108	New Yorker Deluxe	6/3/77
1109	Excel Special	7/9/77
1110	New Yorker Special	9/3/77
1111	12-String Special	11/3/77
1112	New Yorker Special	11/15/77
1113	New Yorker Special	1/27/78
1114	New Yorker Special	12/16/77
1115	New Yorker Deluxe	3/26/78
1116	New Yorker Special	3/18/78
1117	New Yorker Special Oval Hole	5/17/78

D'AQUISTO LEDGER

Number	Model	Date
1118	New Yorker Special	6/1/78
1119	New Yorker Special	6/20/78
1120	New Yorker Special	8/10/78
1121	Excel	8/78
1122	New Yorker Special	10/78
1123	Excel	9/8/78
1124	New Yorker Special	11/12/78
1125	Excel Oval Hole	11/12/78
1126	New Yorker Special, 16"	3/28/79
1127	New Yorker Special	3/15/79
1128	Excel	4/15/79
1129	New Yorker Special	5/15/79
1130	New Yorker Special	9/10/79
1131	New Yorker Special	7/25/79
1132	New Yorker Special	10/9/79
1133	New Yorker Special Jim Hall Model	12/20/79
1134	New Yorker Special	7/24/80
1135	New Yorker Deluxe	3/30/80
1136	New Yorker Special	2/26/80
1137	New Yorker Special	5/15/80
1138	New Yorker Special	5/30/80
1139	New Yorker Special	6/20/80
1140	New Yorker Deluxe 7-String	6/18/80
1141	Excel	10/20/80
1142	New Yorker Special	11/9/80
1143	New Yorker Special Jim Hall	5/10/81
1144	New Yorker Deluxe	2/6/81
1145	New Yorker Deluxe	10/31/80
1146	New Yorker Electric	4/20/81
1147	Excel	1/18/82
1148	New Yorker Special	3/20/82
1149	Excel	1/5/82
1150	New Yorker Special	10/24/81
1151	Electric New Yorker Special	11/17/81
1152	New Yorker Special	4/20/82
1153	New Yorker Special	5/17/82
1154	New Yorker Deluxe	8/25/82
1155	New Yorker Deluxe	6/18/82
1156	New Yorker Special	6/7/82
1157	Excel Special, American Wood	12/20/82
1158	New Yorker Deluxe	8/23/82
1159	Excel	12/13/82
1160	Excel	11/9/82
1161	New Yorker Special	3/29/83
1162	New Yorker Special	7/4/83
1163	New Yorker Special	6/25/83
1164	Special 12-String	12/24/83
1165	New Yorker Deluxe	4/25/84
1166	New Yorker Special	4/30/84
1167	7-String New Yorker Special	5/4/84
1168	New Yorker Deluxe	5/7/84
1169	New Yorker Special	4/18/84
1170	New Yorker Special	8/28/84
1171	Excel	12/20/84
1172*	Excel	8/28/84
1173	3/4 Size Excel	8/27/84
1174	Excel Special	10/84
1175	New Yorker Special	12/20/84
1176	Excel	4/21/85
1177	12-String Classic Oval Hole, 16"	3/20/85
1178	New Yorker Deluxe	4/25/85
1179	New Yorker Deluxe	8/15/85
1180	New Yorker Special	10/24/85

*Listed as an Excel, but it is in fact a New Yorker Oval Hole, 18".

Number	Model	Date
1181	New Yorker Special	9/19/85
1182	Excel	8/15/85
1183	New Yorker Classic, 18″, New	12/17/85
1184	Excel	10/18/86
1185	New Yorker Special	2/22/86
1186	Excel, Non-Cutaway	2/23/86
1187	New Yorker Classic	12/25/86
1188	New Yorker Special	8/20/86
1189	New Yorker Deluxe	10/1/86
1190	New Yorker Special	9/19/86
1191	New Yorker Classic, 17″	11/25/86
1192	New Yorker Special	12/24/86
1193	New Yorker Special	1/5/87
1194	7-String New Yorker Deluxe	12/18/86
1195	New Yorker Special	5/23/87
1196	New Yorker Deluxe	5/13/87
1197	Excel	2/4/88
1198	New Yorker Classic	5/1/87
1199	Excel	8/25/87
1200	Excel	8/16/87
1201	New Yorker Deluxe	1/28/88
1202	New Yorker Special	8/31/87
1203	New Yorker Classic	1/29/88
1204	New Yorker Classic Oval Hole	1/30/88
1205	New Yorker Deluxe	4/8/88
1206	New Yorker Classic	7/24/88
1207	New Yorker Classic Oval Hole, 17″	6/16/88
1208	7-string New Yorker Special	1988
1209	New Yorker Classic	1988
1210	New Yorker Deluxe	1988
1211	25th Anniversary Model D'Aquisto D'Angelico	5/90

Number	Model	Date
1211	New Yorker Classic	1/19/89
1212	"Deco" Avant Garde New Model	1/10/89
1213	New Yorker Special	1/20/89
1214	New Yorker Special	7/5/89
1215	New Yorker Special	7/28/89
1216	New Yorker Classic	8/20/89
1217	New Yorker Special	8/89
1218	Excel	2/22/90
1219	New Yorker Deluxe	2/24/90
1220	Avant Garde 17″	6/29/90
1221	New Yorker Deluxe	7/4/90
1222	Avant Garde	7/2/90
1223	7-string New Yorker Special	7/15/90
1224	Avant Garde	9/90
1225	Excel 12-string	8/27/90
1226	New Yorker Special Jim Hall Model	8/29/90
1227	Classic 18″	9/15/90
1228	New Yorker Special	9/20/90
1229	Excel	9/13/91
1230	Classic 18″	10/8/91
1231	Excel Noncutaway	10/10/91
1232	New Model "Savant" Solo 17″	3/21/92
1233	Solo 17″	4/15/92
1234	Classic	4/21/92
1235	Excel	6/6/92
1236	New Yorker Deluxe	5/4/92
1237	Solo 17″	—
1238	Solo Noncutaway 18″	—
1239	Solo 17″	4/22/93
1241	New Model Centura 17″	3/20/93
1242	Solo Noncutaway 18″	8/10/93
1243	Solo Noncutaway 17″	8/13/93
1244	Centura 17″	8/11/93

Number	Model	Date	Number	Model	Date
1245	Centura 17"	8/14/93	18	—	6/20/79
1246	Solo Special with point	10/93	19	—	7/16/79
1247	Centura 17"	2/23/94	20	—	8/19/79
1248	Avant Garde 18"	10/93	21	—	8/29/79
1249	Centura Deluxe #1 17"	4/1/94	22	—	9/16/79
1250	Solo 17"	5/94	23	—	10/16/79
1251	Centura 17"	8/18/94	24	—	10/30/79
1252	Centura Deluxe 18"	7/94	25	Left-Handed	7/26/80
1253	Centura 17"	1 or 2/95	26	—	9/10/80
1254	Centura 17"	1 or 2/27/95	27	—	10/20/80
1255	"Advance" 18"	11/8/94	28	—	2/15/80
1256	Centura 17"	—	29	—	2/15/80
			30	—	4/15/80
	[CLASSICAL CUTAWAYS]		101	—	7/2/82
101	—	2/20/83	102	—	—
102	—	11/20/86	103	—	—
103	—	1/85	104	Left-Handed	11/20/82
			105	—	8/30/82
	[HOLLOW-BODY ELECTRICS]		106	—	2/12/83
1	—	11/9/76	107	—	3/2/83
2	—	2/10/77	108	—	5/17/83
3	—	5/27/77	109	—	—
4	—	5/12/77	110	—	3/12/85
5	—	7/16/77	111	—	8/20/83
6	—	8/16/77	112	—	12/20/83
7	—	10/27/77	113	—	12/20/84
8	—	11/9/77	114	—	6/12/85
9	—	3/6/78	115	—	—
10	—	5/18/78	116	—	5/15/87
11	—	4/18/79	117	—	2/3/88
12	—	11/9/78	118	—	2/3/88
13	—	12/12/78	119	–	10/20/88
14	—	10/9/78	120	Special Carved-top Acoustic	2/6/89
15	—	7/1/78	121	—	2/3/89
16	—	1/9/79	122	—	2/4/89
17	—	5/25/79	123	—	2/9/90

Number	Model	Date
124	—	5/9/90
125	—	9/28/91
126	—	11/9/91
127	—	—
128	New Model Centura	3/1/94
129	—	6/12/94
130	—	7/16/94
131	—	3/31/95
132	—	4/1/95

[SOLIDS & HOLLOW SOLIDS]

Number	Model	Date
E101	—	1976
E102	7-String	12/27/76
E103	—	3/12/77
E104	—	5/1/78
E105	—	5/10/78
E106	—	8/3/78
E107	—	3/30/79
E108	7-String	10/30/79
E109	—	11/19/79
E110	—	8/27/80
E111	—	9/6/80
E112	—	11/9/81
E113	—	4/20/82
E114	—	—
E115	Special Curved Back	3/28/83
E116	New Design Double Cutaway "Americus"	8/28/83
E117	—	3/12/84
E118	Double Cutaway	4/25/85
E119	New "Sonorous" Model #1	8/21/85
E120	—	11/9/85
E121	Double Cutaway	1/86
E122	—	5/1/87
E123	Sinclavier	5/1/87
124	Left-Handed	6/24/88

Number	Model	Date
125	—	1/89
126	—	1/89
127	—	2/90
128	Left-Handed	3/90
129	—	6/17/91

[CENTURA MODELS]

Number	Model	Date
1001	Spruce Top	12/28/93
1002	Maple Top	12/28/93
1003	Blue Double Cutaway	11/9/94
1004	Red Single Cutaway	12/25/94
1005	Single Cutaway Spruce Top	2/12/95

[FLAT-TOPS]

Number	Model	Date
101	Special 15" Short Body	1/73
102	Deluxe 16" Full Body	10/25/75
103	Deluxe 16"	6/12/76
104	Deluxe 16"	4/18/77
105	Deluxe 16"	9/10/77
106	Deluxe 16"	2/10/78
107	Deluxe 16"	12/20/78
108	Deluxe 16"	6/20/79
109	Deluxe 16"	12/18/79
110	Deluxe 16"	12/20/80
111	Deluxe 16"	2/20/81
112	16" Special Short Body	4/13/81
113	Small Cutaway	5/20/81
114	Small Cutaway	11/3/81
115	Small Cutaway	3/3/83
116	Deluxe 16"	6/83

[MANDOLINS]

Number	Model	Date
101	—	—
102	—	—
103	—	—

Sources of Additional Information

FILM

Cohen, Frederick. *The New Yorker Special: Handcrafting a Guitar.* 16mm. 28 min. 1986. Available from the Filmmakers Library, 124 East 40th St., New York, NY 10016.

MAGAZINE ARTICLES

Andersen, Steven. "1948 D'Angelico New Yorker." *American Lutherie*, no. 16 (Winter 1988): 29–32.

Bernard, Joe. "Chords of Gold." *Sky Magazine*, September 1990, 40–50.

Carlin, Richard. "In Praise of Arch-Tops." *Frets*, October 1986, 26–32.

D'Aquisto, James L. "Some Thoughts and Stories from the 1978 Convention Lecture." *The Guild of American Luthiers Quarterly* 7, no. 2 (June 1979): 14–16.

———. "An Interview with James D'Aquisto." Parts 1–3. *Guitarmaker* (The Association of Stringed Instrument Artisans), no. 9, 10, 12. (October 1990, December 1990, June 1991): 18–25, 9–13, 21–22; 15–17, 23–24, 28–34.

Gill, Chris. "James D'Aquisto." *Guitar Player*, August 1995, 38–39.

Johnston, Richard. "Archtop Artistry." *Acoustic Guitar*, March/April 1994, 44–54.

Landgarten, Ira. "D'Aquisto." *Frets*, December 1980, 10, 12.

Olsen, Tim. "Luthier Jimmy D'Aquisto." *Guitar Player*, September 1978, 40–41, 112, 114.

———. "James L. D'Aquisto: Building the Archtop Guitar." *American Lutherie* (quarterly journal of the Guild of American Luthiers), no. 37 (Spring 1994): 6–20.

Rozek, Michael. "A Craftsman of Note." *Quest*, October 1988, 30–32.

———. "Luthier Deluxe." *Creative Living*, Winter 1991, 19–21.

"The Talk of the Town: Exceptional." *The New Yorker*, 29 January 1990, 27–28.

Van Hoose, Tom, Jay Scott, Lawrence Acunto, Steve Miller, "James L. D'Aquisto." *20th Century Guitar* 5, no. 5 (June 1995): 110–118.

Yelin, Robert. "D'Aquisto Carrys [sic] on in the D'Angelico Tradition." *Guitar Player*, February 1970, 28–30.

BOOKS

Chinnery, Scott, and Tony Bacon. "The Chinnery Collection: 150 Years of American Guitars." 1996.

Evans, Tom, and Mary Anne Evans. "Guitars." New York: Facts On File, 1977.

Gruhn, George, and Walter Carter. "Acoustic Guitars and Other Fretted Instruments." GPI Books, 1993.

Hill, W. Henry, Arthur F. Hill, and Alfred E. Hill. "Antonio Stradivari, His Life and Work (1644–1737)." New York: Dover Publications, Inc., 1963.

Mongan, Norman. "The History of the Guitar in Jazz." New York: Oak Publications, 1983.

Sloane, Irving. "Steel String Guitar Construction." New York: Dutton—Sunrise Inc., 1975.

Tsumura, Akira. "Guitars: The Tsumura Collection." Kodansha International, 1987.

Van Hoose, Thomas A. "The Gibson Super 400: Art of the Fine Guitar." GPI Books, 1991.

Wheeler, Tom. "American Guitars: An Illustrated History." New York: Harper Perennial, 1982 and 1990.

Index

Amati, 54, 59, 130
Ampeg, 6, 18
Andersen, Steven, 60, 100
Antone, Anthony, 70, 73, 82, 84
Archaic String Company, 131
Appollon, Dave, 140–141

Bauer, Billy, 145
Bay, Mel, 73, 156
Bell Hops, The, 83
Berg Company, 70
Bigsby Company, 68

Chenet, Al, 84
Ciani, 5–6, 30
Code Company, 40
Cohen, Frederick, 82, 107

D'Addario String Company, 131, 133
Danelectro Company, 18–19, 141
Darco String Company, 131
DeArmond Company, 68
DeMarco, Don, 92
DiSerio, Vincent, 5, 8, 15–17, 20–22, 50, 53, 85–86, 88
Duchin, Peter, 144

Empire State Building, 64
Epiphone Company, 6, 20, 57, 147

Farlow, Tal, 82
Favilla Guitar Company, 6, 17, 21, 84, 88
Fender Corporation, 100, 134
Frosali, Mario, 5, 7

Gibson Guitar Company, 5–6, 20, 30, 36, 40, 45, 47, 56–57, 59, 62, 64, 69–70, 84, 103, 126, 128, 147
Gretsch Company, 9
Grover Company, 65, 69
Gruhn, George, 147
Guarneri, 45
Guild of American Luthiers, ix, 107

Hagstrom Company, 127, 132
Hall, Jim, 82, 156
Henderson, Fletcher, 39
Henderson, Skitch, 144

Jay, Stan, 146

Lang, Eddie, 73, 149
Louis Handel Company, 63
Lyon & Healy Company, 47–48

Martin Guitar Company, 125
Melanie, 124
Melega, George, 143

Micro–Flex String Company, 132
Monteleone, John, 33, 55
Moore, Oscar, 53
Mortel, Benny, 9

Osborne, Mary, 142

Paganini, 48
Puma, Joe, 82

Rainey, Jimmy, 82
Reichman, Joe, 139
Rundquist, Freddie, 147

Schaffner, Joseph, 63, 66
Sebring, David, 149
Shearing, George, 40, 69

Smith, Johnny, 11, 13, 41, 67–68, 87, 142, 156
Stradivari, 59, 121, 129, 130, 143
Thielemans, Toots, 69

Umanov, Matt, 144
United Guitars, 11, 17, 40, 127

Valenti, Al, 6, 9–11, 19, 30, 75, 138–139
Valesquez, Emmanuel, 20
Victor, Frank, 73
Volpe, Harry, 73

Waverly Company, 69
Wayne, Chuck, 40
Wexer, Lawrence, 45, 147

About the Author

Paul William Schmidt was born in 1958 in Waverly, Iowa. He has taught privately and at the collegiate level, and served as assistant director of the National Music Center. He holds a bachelor's degree in music theory from Wartburg College, a master of music degree in education from Pacific Lutheran University, and a master of divinity degree in theology from Trinity Lutheran Seminary. He has received grants from the National Endowment for the Humanities and the Selmer Corporation, and has written articles for various music magazines. His other books include *The History of the Ludwig Drum Company*, and *Routes of Rock—a Course of Study for Post–WWII Western European and African-based Vernacular Dance and Art Music*. He has also released four albums of original music and lyrics. He continues his creative, artistic, and theological endeavors in the Midwest, where he lives with his wife, two children, and dog.